TREK AIRWAYS
A South African Adventure

TREK AIRWAYS
A South African Adventure

William Buckland Rorke

ATHENA PRESS
LONDON

TREK AIRWAYS
A South African Adventure
Copyright © William Buckland Rorke 2007

All Rights Reserved

No part of this book may be reproduced in any form
by photocopying or by any electronic or mechanical means,
including information storage or retrieval systems,
without permission in writing from both the copyright
owner and the publisher of this book.

ISBN 10-digit: 1 84401 858 X
ISBN 13-digit: 978 1 84401 858 1

First Published 2007 by
ATHENA PRESS
Queen's House, 2 Holly Road
Twickenham TW1 4EG
United Kingdom

Printed for Athena Press

To Bryan Oriel Rorke
whose generosity has made this publication possible

Acknowledgements

Many thanks to the following people and organisations, without whom this book would not be illustrated with such wonderful photographs: John Foggitt, Mimi Coertse, Pretoria Archives, Pretoria Boys High, Sabine von Mellenthin and South African Airways Museum.

Thanks also to John Austin-Williams, Peter Jackson, Lorbrand (Pty) Ltd, Therese Els of Constania Park Library, Janice Farquharson, Jackie van Lingen of Seeff Properties and Helena Labuschagne.

Contents

Prologue	11
Author's Tribute to John Gledhill Foggitt	
A Pen Picture	13
Introduction	15
Sydney Excel	18
African Air Safaris	22
Rodney Rooken-Smith	23
Phoenix Airlines	24
Phoenix's Inaugural Flights	26
The Birth of Trek Airways	28
Tropic Airways	29
Fanie Botha	37
William Edward Hamilton (Jock), DSO, DFC	43
William Buckland Rorke (Paddy)	46
Sydney Excel	52
Tom Meredith	54
Fred Gratz	55
General Helm von Mellenthin	57
Board Rumblings	58
Flight Schedules and Service	60
Administration	66

Bombshell	70
Pongola Sugar Estates	71
Exit Fanie Botha	72
Aircraft Re-equipment	75
Chairman	76
John Foggitt and TFC	77
Jock Hamilton and the Safari Club	80
Four Engines	85
Apartheid Sanctions	87
Joggie Vermooten – Rentmeester Beleggings Bpk	90
Minister Ben Schoeman & Danie Joubert	93
Diversions	97
Trek/Luxavia Philosophy	99
Safmarine	100
The Demise	102
The Years After	107
The Aircraft	108
The Passengers	114
Trek's Side Issues	127
Trek's Directors	129
The Years That Might Have Been	131
Jock, in His Own Words	133
William Buckland 'Paddy' Rorke	146

Obituary: Friederich von Mellenthin,	
Rommel's Chief of Intelligence	173
A Tribute to William Buckland Rorke (Paddy)	176
Requiem	178
Epilogue	179

Prologue

Unless a person is directly involved in the task of starting and building an airline, unless he has lived through the almost impossible obstacles that stand in the way of such a venture, it is almost beyond imagination to absorb the problems that beset such an adventure. To the directors, the executives and staff who stuck by this difficult task must go the highest accolades for, in those far-off days, when aviation was in its extreme infancy, each new problem would have turned away anyone but the most fiercely determined executive. To get traffic rights, to find the aircraft, to fix the rights en route and the night-stops required to fly up Africa, were all massive tasks. Then to find passengers to board this tiny aircraft to spend three nights at random stops was still another whole exercise. I salute these tough men who soldiered on undaunted, as I was in almost daily contact with them as I used their ever-growing services. This book tells only a fraction of the story but records a giant step in the development of the airline industry in South Africa.

John G Foggitt

Around the Corner

Around the corner I have a friend,
In this great city that has no end,
Yet days go by and weeks rush on
And before I know it a year is gone,
And I never see my old friend's face
For Life is a swift and terrible race.
He knows I like him just as well
As in the days when I rang his bell
And he rang mine. We were younger then,
And now we are busy, tired men –

Tired with playing a foolish game,
Tired with trying to make a name.
'Tomorrow,' I say, 'I will call on Jim.'
But tomorrow comes – and tomorrow goes
As the tide of life it ebbs and flows;
Around the corner, yet miles away.
'Here's a telegram sir – Jim died today!'
And that's what we get – and deserve in the end –
Around the corner, a vanished friend.

J G F, 1982

Author's Tribute to John Gledhill Foggitt: A Pen Picture

J G Foggitt is a man of resource, courage and expertise – he is indeed a character!

He started his career as a humdrum civil servant. At an early age he married and raised a family. His innate spirit of adventure and drive could not long be denied. After years of useful service he resigned his safe and promising job to fulfil a need which he saw in his country – new blood for South Africa! He launched his South African Immigration Organisation (Samorgan). During the regime of General Smuts' United Party, Samorgan was instrumental in bringing to the country 22,000 immigrants, mostly young men from war-torn Europe. The developing mines of the Orange Free State were crying out for new blood to cope with the boom in the gold market. The advent of the apartheid nationalist government saw immigration being severely curbed. John turned his attention to travel. He told me that he was forming a 'joke club', to be called the Travellers' Facilities Club (TFC). His aim was to provide comfortable travel for the holiday-minded at an affordable cost. How well he succeeded was borne out by the thousands of travellers both in South Africa and also in overseas countries, who flocked to book conducted tours to all corners of the globe to enjoy faraway places which they hitherto had never been able to afford. His monthly newsletters were devoured by thousands of his devotees, and every concluding poem (that he had written himself) was so popular that he later published many of them in book form.

TFC became a household name!

When his two sons matriculated, another side of John's character was revealed. To ensure that they would not fall prey to drugs or television inertia, he settled them on a tract of land in northernmost Alaska in America. The plan was for them to learn the value of exercising initiative and independence by farming in an isolated area completely cut off from civilisation during the snowbound long winter months. After several years they returned, reliant and resourceful young men, to join John in developing his various business enterprises, and particularly TFC. A lesson to all modern parents!

For many years, TFC flourished until John decided to devote his energies to pastures new. His successors could not match the enterprise and expertise of John G Foggitt, and the organisation eventually folded.

Today, well into his eighties, John still refuses to retire gracefully. His spirit still urges him on, and even as I write, he is preparing to fulfil a lifelong dream. Next month (February 2002), he is set to visit one of the few places in the world where he has not yet set foot – he is about to board a ship bound for the freezing South Pole.

What a man! What an octogenarian! A true son of South Africa.

Introduction

It was with tears in my eyes that I read in the *Pretoria News* on Tuesday, 12 April 1994 of the demise of Flight Star, originally known as Trek Airways. My mind went back forty years to 24 September 1953, when I gained the certificate of Incorporation of Trek Airways (Pty) Ltd.

This is a fragment of South African history in the latter twentieth century. It is the story of a goal reached by a handful of young enthusiasts – some not so young, some not even South Africans – two Brits, one German and five South Africans.

This is a tribute to the single-mindedness of the coterie – men with imagination, drive, resourcefulness, with an entrepreneurial spirit and willing to take chances yet without being reckless or foolhardy – just like the original trekkers in South Africa of old.

It was the end and it was the beginning. It was Hitler's war, and it was this war which was the end and also the beginning. It was the end of bombs and V2s and it was the beginning of flying for joy and reward – no longer for vengeance and retaliation.

VE Day in 1945. Suddenly there arose, on the one hand, an army of wing-breasted men yearning for their flying years never to stop. On the other hand, there was a body of well-heeled entrepreneurs with their hands in their pockets and greed in their eyes – just waiting for the new flying era to begin. Now they too would be part of it – the profit would be theirs.

No wonder that in South Africa, as indeed in so many other countries, there arose a National Transport Commission (NTC) with a mandate to supervise, control and regularise the new bubble about to burst upon society – the airline industry, both nationally and internationally. Even before the half-century was reached the NTC had granted eight licences for private charter flying – licences to companies with no experience in airline operation. The companies were composed of fighting airmen who had now donned airline uniforms, discarded aircraft taken out of mothballs from wartime and financiers with eyes only on profit. The travel-starved populace flocked to explore the wonders of holidays and business abroad. Those who for six weary war years had found fear from overhead, now experienced the joy and wonder of winging their way through tranquil skies. The air boom had started.

But alas! As the fifties dawned, so fingers were burnt and mushrooming airlines began to learn bitter lessons. They realised that even talented and highly experienced aviators could not sustain without the cooperation of skilled, honest and capable businessmen – businessmen ready to dig deep into their pockets. These two factors had to work together in harmony, understanding and trust, in a mutual spirit of give and take.

This just did not happen. Our story begins in 1949, a mere four years after the war. It was a time for brave men to readjust to civilian life, to hang out their DSOs and DRCs to dry, and to look for a future livelihood. There were aviators without wings to fly, and there were aircraft by the thousands being put into mothballs or simply discarded. No wonder that some few began to put disused crafts back into action – but this time not to pulverise the enemy, rather to give service to a travel-starved public. Would-be airlines arose in South Africa – at least seven. But always it was the same story: the enterprise was started by magnificent wartime pilots, but they had no clue of commercial or financial technique.

Sometimes it was the reverse: enthusiastic capitalists with business know-how, but with no experience of controlling prima donna-ish aircrews or army-orientated engineers. In all seven cases the result was inevitable – disaster and liquidation. By 1953 all but one of the aspirant air services had either folded or stood on the point of bankruptcy. But one remained, using General Smuts' wartime Avro York, now out of mothballs and no longer on martial missions, but instead carrying gold and passengers to Europe for reward. This airline was Tropic Airways. However in 1952, Sydney Excel, Rodney Rooken-Smith and Paddy Rorke met in Pretoria to lay the foundations of Trek Airways. Mad dogs we undoubtedly were, but dreamers too – and sometimes dreams can come true. Our dream came true – and was certainly rewarding.

Perhaps, however, we should go back a few years. In actual

fact it all began, strictly speaking, in 1949 with Syd Excel – a fine figure of a man: always dapper, always with a white shirt, shorts and very neat stockings together with a cane – but always allergic to any work that was not to do with aviation.

Sydney Excel

Sydney Excel was as bizarre a character as ever was. He had a pleasing appearance and a unique way of attracting people to him. This, despite his devil-may-care, 'don't give a damn' outlook on life, his almost complete disregard for anything resembling hard work and his argumentative unreasonableness, bordering on the lunatic. He was very likeable when normal, but a vicious beast when roused. But that was Syd – Jekyll and Hyde. In his immaculate shorts, gartered stockings, well-pressed shirt and light cane, he could well have been Bill Clinton at Camp David or Beau Brummell on vacation.

He first came into my life (or rather, shall I say, my wife, Ticatic's, life) when one day I came home from work. Ticatic said, 'I met one of our neighbours.' He was boarding with our opposite neighbour in fashionable Waterkloof. Perhaps boarding is too euphemistic a word – I am sure it was rather as a non-paying guest, although I never really found out. It seemed to me barely possible that his modest income could have covered the style of life that Rients Turkstra lavished upon him. Perhaps I was wrong.

Hats off to Syd, who throughout my association with him always contrived to 'land with his bum in the butter'. A guardian angel he definitely had! He was a physical fitness fanatic, a long-distance swimmer (he once swam across the Bosphorus) and a one-time big game hunter and guide. Over a drink in our lounge one day he made a startling statement – not unusual for him. 'Tomorrow my name will be on the front page of the *Pretoria News*.' Just like that! He would say no more. 'You will see tomorrow.'

Sure enough, in the *Pretoria News*, there were front-page headlines reading, 'Fanatic tries to murder Elliot Wilson, Chief Director of Flying'. This article explained how an unknown man (later identified as Syd Excel) entered Elliot Wilson's office by appointment, drew a revolver and shouted, 'Are you going to renew my airline transport licence?' He then fired two shots to the left and to the right of a terrified Elliot Wilson, threw the revolver on the desk, opened the door to admit two detectives and calmly said to them, 'Arrest me,' which they did.

He refused bail and spent weeks in Pretoria Central Prison awaiting trial. This is how he explained his extraordinary action.

'At the outbreak of the war in 1939 I was in the police force. Naturally I volunteered immediately and was drafted into the tank corps. This was my chance to fulfil my life's ambition to become a pilot. From the very beginning I repeatedly applied for transfer to the air force, but was always refused. In frustration I organised a sit-down strike amongst the recruits who were all furious at having messing charges each day deducted from their pay packets. I was the ringleader, and in order to break the strike, I was immediately drafted up north.

'As soon as I was settled in the desert camp, I again began pestering to be transferred to the air force. By now I was dubbed a troublemaker and all my requests fell on deaf ears. In desperation I again went on a sit-down strike – a one-man strike. I got detention and later solitary confinement. I went on a starving campaign and refused all food. After a few days the OC (Officer Commanding) wanted to wash his hands of me, and I was sent back to Pretoria to Weskoppies Asylum.

'Here I stayed for many weeks and during that time I wrote to the Prime Minister, Jannie Smuts, asking for my case to be reviewed. A Board of Enquiry was appointed and eventually I was exonerated and allowed to transfer to the air force – I had won! But, alas, I had made a bitter enemy of the Superintendent of Weskoppies. I was in the habit of doing all my daily exercises behind the iron fences and while busy one morning, the Superintendent arrived and said he had noted my unusual routine – "Who do you think you are – Adonis?" he said. I immediately replied, "Well, I'm not a pot-bellied bastard like you." This remark made him my enemy for life and his report when I was discharged stayed with me for years after. The report read: "In my opinion Excel is not a fit person to be in command of a passenger plane."

'In the air force I got my wings and flew transport planes throughout the war. Back in Civvy Street I had to earn a living – the police force was for the birds! So I applied for an airline transport licence, only to be turned down time after time. "Excel is not a fit person to be in charge of a passenger plane" – the shadow of the superintendent's report at Weskoppies still hung over me.

'No one was prepared to listen to my story about Weskoppies and so, in desperation, I wrote again to General Jan Smuts (as he was then) – the Prime Minister. I received no reply and so I wrote to Elliot Wilson, Chief Director of Flying – no satisfaction. And that is the reason I went to his office that day and shot at Elliot. As mentioned previously there was no intention to do him any bodily harm but just to get a hearing, and that was why I landed up in prison.'

That was Syd Excel's story why he landed up in prison. He had been adamant that he would conduct his own defence and needed no legal assistance. *Mirabile dictu*! The judge listened to his case, sympathised with him and gave him a nominal fine for pointing a firearm, and ordered that his flying licence be restored. Syd had again triumphed through perseverance. He had got his wings again.

At about this time (1950), many wartime pilots in search of work had obtained licences to operate aircraft for gain (this was just after the war), but already seven such quasi-airlines had ended in bankruptcy and liquidation. One was still operating, and very successfully too, between South Africa and Europe. This was Tropic Airways.

Syd, with his newly acquired wings, signed on with Tropic, doing two to three flights per month as second officer. After each flight he would walk across the street to me and regale my family with stories of overseas places. The war had naturally prevented our family and many other people from any overseas travel. He had told us many stories about his flying experiences. For example, after the armistice he had stayed on for a considerable period in the air force, carrying out various transportation chores – the Berlin airlift, ferrying displaced persons back to their homelands. He always used to smile as he related to us some of these experiences. On one occasion he told us about a flight taking evacuees back to their home in Armenia, when he smelt fire on board. Inspection showed that his passengers had felt cold and had started a newspaper fire. Panic – but it was soon extinguished.

On another occasion, his aircraft had run out of fuel over the Mediterranean. He did a belly landing and dived into the sea, only to find that he was in only three feet of water. He waded ashore and gave thanks to his guardian angel!

Once, as a temporary measure, he joined in the conduct of shooting safaris, usually in Africa, north of the Limpopo. His training in the police, as well as some of his experiences in Spain, had made him an excellent shot. Besides, he was at home in the bush. This form of employment was only spasmodic, but it gave him a taste for hunting safaris. It also gave him plenty of time to dream. It was with these dreams that one day he approached me with what he thought was a master scheme.

African Air Safaris

He told me that he visualised bringing small but elite parties of game hunters to Africa, and providing them with comfort and luxury in the veld (bush). He envisaged small groups of wealthy Americans visiting and being given home comforts in the bush – carpets in the tents, whisky on tap and well-prepared meals. Many would be big game hunters who would be prepared to spend money like water in order to shoot a lion or an elephant; expense would be no object. Further, instead of laborious journeys by jeep into the wilds, the star attraction would be that all transport would be done in comfortable, reliable aircraft. The trip would last for one month, the party would consist of only about ten would-be trophy hunters, and he reckoned that a charge of £10,000 would be quite acceptable – especially to stars from Hollywood who were always in search of adventure. Syd said that three or even two parties each year would easily be filled and would bring a handsome profit. Furthermore there would be months of relaxation between trips which would mean months of leisure – a lovely thought for Sydney Excel. He even had a name for the enterprise: 'African Air Safaris'.

Syd's proposition to me was that as he sought finance and also a financial advisor to keep the books, would I come in? I was not really impressed by the financial viability of his scheme and in any case I had no spare cash for such an investment. I promised to keep an eye open for a likely entrepreneur. In my own mind I had written the proposition off.

Rodney Rooken-Smith

A strange quirk of fate was later to bring Syd's scheme back to mind. Ticatic and I decided to take a short holiday cruise from Durban to Cape Town. Little did we realise that this jaunt would turn out to be an historic occasion, altering our lives for ever. We were relaxing on the luxury liner at sea when we bumped into an interesting character – a retired big game hunter from Kenya called Rodney Rooken-Smith. He was only in his mid-thirties, and had come to the Union to seek a vocation. He had had enough of big game hunting in Central Africa. He reminded us a lot of Syd Excel – a pleasing appearance, quietly spoken, but certainly more refined than our Syd, without his moods and tantrums. He was a most likeable man. He had war experience of flying, and had kept his licence up to date by acting as pilot for hunting safaris in Central Africa, while he was also good as a hunting guide. He was a man of parts, who had accumulated a fair amount of capital.

When I said that we bumped into Rod, it was not quite that way. He had spotted Ticatic and was immediately another bee round the honey pot. I think he rather regarded me as a somewhat unnecessary appendage. Nevertheless, we three frequently consorted over cocktails. Naturally in due course I had to mention Syd's African Air Safaris. To my amazement Rod immediately embraced the idea – it was just the sort of thing that he was looking for. He promised to come to Pretoria to meet the redoubtable Sydney Excel.

When we left the ship at Cape Town I had already discarded Rod's interest in Syd's scheme. I was wrong.

To my amazement, soon after our return, we found Rod on our doorstep in Pretoria. To this day I still do not know which was the bigger attraction – Ticatic or Syd's baby. However his arrival heralded the birth of African Air Safaris (AAS).

Phoenix Airlines

Rodney and Syd clicked immediately and African Air Safaris became a reality, with myself a reluctant member. Rod agreed to provide working capital of £3,000, provided both Syd and I came in as equal partners and each guaranteed £1,000. I registered African Air Safaris (Pty) Ltd in the Pretoria Companies office in 1949. We drew up elaborate, coloured brochures with details of big game hunting in Africa and despatched them to travel agents in the Union and also in California. But we still had one major problem – where to charter an aircraft suitable for carrying ten passengers as well as their shooting accoutrements.

Fortune smiled on me. In conversation with a good attorney friend of mine I learned that he was in the process of establishing an airline to operate out of Wonderboom Airport in Pretoria. They would be using two Douglas DC-2 planes imported from Swissair, each taking fourteen passengers. Furthermore they were still short of £3,000 investment capital – just the amount being put up by Rod. We were in. We drew up a contract with their new company, Phoenix Airlines (Pty) Ltd, whereby AAS could at any time charter one of the DC-2s for a reasonable fee. AAS was in business, and I found myself on the board of Phoenix. I, whose sole experience in the air was during the war when I rashly agreed to a flight in a fighter plane doing a dive-bombing exercise. In the two-seater fighter I sat back-to-back with the pilot, looking nervously as the tail went up and down in the manoeuvre. The drill was that the pilot had to climb to 5,000 feet and then dive straight on to a target marked out on the ground, releasing a volley of bullets at the target and pulling out quickly at 200 feet so as not to crash into the ground. All very terrifying for a novice like me on my first flight. To make matters worse, the pilot jammed his machine gun and was not allowed to land before emptying his magazine. Instead of the usual five circuits, he was obliged to go round fifteen times. How I lived through it I shall never know. It cost me five shillings to have the plane cleaned out, as well as a new pair of underpants. Never again! Yet here I was, now a director of an airline – life can be funny. This was not really the recommended initial training for an embryo director.

The delivery of the two aircraft from Swissair had now to take place. Syd was deputed to fetch one from Switzerland and a friend of mine, Vyv Graham, the other. On a joyful day the shareholders of Phoenix gathered at Wonderboom Airport to witness the aircrafts' arrival. Phoenix was on its way.

Phoenix's Inaugural Flights

With the arrival of the DC-2, Phoenix got down to business. I was very soon to learn that running an airline concern is as hazardous as negotiating a field of landmines. The first problem the Phoenix board faced was that we had two full loads of passengers southbound, but not a single passenger northbound – in Europe winter was setting in and who in South Africa wanted to be there? Syd undertook to find northbound freight, which he did. There were two loads of karakul skins to be picked up in Windhoek – our problem was solved. I should at this stage mention that we had put an extra row of seats into the two DC-2s, converting them from 21-seaters to 28-seaters, to make them more profitable.

On a fine sunny day both planes took off for Windhoek – at last Phoenix was in the air. Little did we expect what was to follow. I was doing an audit in Warmbaths when the news came through. One plane, piloted by one of our directors, Bob Peace, had landed in a mealie field near Bulawayo – out of fuel. The other plane was piloted by Vyv Graham and would have to turn back to uplift a spare tail-wheel which was on Bob's aircraft. It was essential that the DC-2 carry a spare tail-wheel. To avoid unnecessary delay, Vyv came back, picked up the wheel and was again on his way. Syd was acting as co-pilot to Vyv and persuaded him to press on to Khartoum even though night was falling. Syd said we could not arrive late for our passengers (pax). Our board had expressly forbade any night flying over the African jungles – too dangerous with only twin-engined aircraft. Backed by Syd, Vyv chose to ignore this instruction, and flew into the night. They arrived safely at Khartoum, but were shattered to learn that the airport was closed due to a desert sandstorm.

Vyv was in a serious quandary – there was not sufficient fuel to go much further. Luckily, he had done plenty of wartime flying in the area, and remembered a landing strip used during the war at Kosti, on the confluence of the White and Blue Nile rivers. It was their only hope. In the black African night, in Stygian darkness, he did well to locate the runway. After three dummy runs he essayed a blind landing – helped only by an African holding a hurricane lantern on the ground. It was a perfect landing, but unfortunately the port side of the aircraft was torn away by a windsock, which was unseen, on the side of the runway. The navigator, Bill Fortuin, was killed instantly, as was the company auditor who was a passenger. He refused to use his seat belt, and broke his neck in a fall from the plane. Vyv had a deep gash in one leg, which in later years caused his death. Syd's guardian angel looked after him – he came out unscathed.

Thus in one day on their inaugural flights, both Phoenix aircraft were write-offs. It was only when we sent relief planes that we learned the awful truth of the accidents. A DC-3 (bigger than a DC-2) was sent to pick up and deliver the karakul skins. When the relief plane was fully loaded there still remained a large quantity of skins over. There had obviously been a hopeless overload. Only later did the board discover what had happened. Syd had cut the freight charge for the skins to the bone. In order to make it financially viable he had cooked the load sheets, showing kilos instead of pounds.

No wonder they could not take on sufficient fuel. The aircraft insurers refused to pay for the damaged planes, Phoenix was insolvent and both Phoenix and AAS were liquidated.

Syd's dream of air safaris went up in smoke and I was finished with aviation – or so I thought. We lost our £3,000.

The Birth of Trek Airways

It is said that time heals all things. For Sydney Excel it took no time at all to get over the Phoenix debacle. It did not seem to enter his ken that his perfidy in the overload had indirectly caused the two crashes. The excess weight had resulted in less than full fuel tanks, to comply with overall weight requirements. Not only the loss of two young lives, but also the financial loss of the investors was as water off a duck's back for Syd. The rest of us were so downhearted that it did not ever occur to us to inform the *Guinness Book of Records* of undoubtedly the shortest airline lifetime in aviation history – a mere few months.

Our Syd was not only tenacious and persistent, but also more resilient than an elastic rubber ball. Without even waiting a respectful period after the Phoenix funeral, he was again at Rod and myself. 'Phoenix has taught us how not to run an airline. They were nothing but monkeys. The only remaining airline operating a charter service to Europe is Tropic Airways, and their three directors are fighting between themselves. Worse than the feud between the United party and the Nationalists in our politics. The way is open for a new licence and it must be ours.' He then gave us the low-down on the affairs of Tropic Airways.

Tropic Airways

Being at a loose end after the demise of Phoenix, Syd had managed to get a part-time job flying now and then as second dickey for Tropic. As usual he poked his nose into the history of the airline. Tropic Airways was an interesting set-up. It consisted of three entrepreneurs: Harry Creed, Tom Meredith and Jock Hamilton. Tom and Jock were both British (although Jock always insisted that he was Scottish). Both had seen war service in the Royal Air Force in the war. Tom had been an English policeman who joined up and was lucky enough to survive hostilities while flying bomber aircraft. Jock joined up from Scotland, but could not get his full wings as his heart had a murmur. He was accepted as a navigator and wireless operator (wop). He was awarded the DFC (Distinguished Flying Cross) – a single and unusual honour for a navigator. This was typical of Jock throughout his whole lifetime – a man to be admired.

After being demobbed Jock met up with Tom and tried to earn a living by opening a travel agency called Meredair. They did well enough to open a branch office in Johannesburg, where they had both been during service. There they met up with Harry Creed, a South African war pilot who was busy establishing a charter service to Europe using General Jan Smuts' wartime personal plane – an Avro York. Creed was searching for partners, and so Tom and Jock joined his Tropic Air. Jock provided half the capital, £500, but allowed Tom a 40% share, retaining only 10% for himself.

Tropic entered the field at a propitious time when others had failed and soon its planes were flying very profitably with passengers and occasional loads of gold.

Tropic Airways (Pty) Ltd had been floated in Johannesburg in 1950. The directors, as noted, were Harry Creed, Jock Hamilton and Tom Meredith. Fred Gratz, who had a wealth of aircraft maintenance experience during the war and then with SAA, was appointed company engineer, and what a hardworking, knowledgeable and talented engineer he was! From the start the company had made profits quite unlike the other similar would-be airlines that had mushroomed after the war, only to be liquidated in double quick time. The trouble with these airlines was that they had been started by ex-air force pilots with no commercial know-how, or by enthusiastic financiers with no flying know-how. Consequently they could only fail. Tropic Airways had good reliable pilots and good engineering facilities. Besides, Harry Creed as chairman had some business instinct. The company flourished, the aircraft was paid off and there was a healthy bank balance. Only Harry Creed and Tom Meredith were stationed in Johannesburg whilst Jock Hamilton ran the commercial side. The finances were good, the bank balance built up, but alas, there was bad feeling creeping in between the directors. Harry Creed was a difficult personality, nicknamed 'Little Hitler' – a veritable dictator. This eventually got under the skins of both Tom and Jock – so much so that on one fine day when Harry was taking a flight to Europe, they decided to apply to the Supreme Court in Johannesburg for an order of judicial management – not for financial matters, but only because the board could no longer control the affairs of the company due to a rift in the directorate. They wanted an outside judicial manager to be appointed. On his return Creed was furious and tried unsuccessfully to oppose the court order. The creditors, as well as the bank manager of Tropic, became dubious – the rot started to set in.

This whole history Syd related to Rod and me. Tropic, he said, would not last and the field would be wide open for a new charter operator. We must not miss this chance. Rod and I hoped to stop his continual pestering by agreeing to join him in yet another air venture if he could raise the necessary capital. We thought this would shut him up. But we underestimated our Syd. He introduced us to Fanie Botha. Another chapter had begun. And so it came about that Syd suggested that we travel to Heidelberg in the Transvaal to meet Fanie. Syd made the arrangements for the meeting to take place in a cafe.

I was not convinced but had privately remarked to Rod, 'Perhaps we had better humour the bugger.' Fanie Botha we had never heard of except that Syd said he was a 'good *ou*'.[1] Apparently they had met on various safaris. So it was in a small cafe in Heidelberg that Syd introduced us to Fanie. We could not help but be impressed by his rugged appearance, his undoubted good looks and his forthright and confident manner of speech.

However, at that stage, Fanie Botha did not want to be bothered with our licence application, although he had guaranteed us £15,000 by way of a loan. As we set about preparing our new licence application, I suggested that African Air Safaris (Pty) Ltd was not a suitable title for an international airline. We all agreed to find a more catchy name. My contention was that it should be short, descriptive and bilingual (for our future South African customers). I put forward the name 'Trek', which they both accepted.

After a few preliminaries, Fanie said, 'Yes, I like Syd's idea. I tell you what – I am prepared to advance £15,000 for a quarter share, provided that I am managing director and chairman of Trek – also that I have notarial bond over the plane. Furthermore, I shall approach the Minister of Defence, a mate of mine, to release to us a redundant Douglas DC-3 Dakota – I am sure he will agree to put one up for tender and we can pick it up for a song.' The deed was done – Syd had confounded us both. We had never expected to be so excited about Syd's madcap plan – but the presence of Fanie gave the whole proposition a sense of reality.

The procedure agreed upon was that Fanie would approach the minister as soon as possible, but it might take a little while before the auction could be arranged – it would first have to be advertised in the *Government Gazette*. In the meantime I was deputed to register the company Trek Airways (Pty) Ltd. It was also agreed that I would appear before the NTC (National Transport Commission) to apply for a licence to fly to Europe and the UK.

It was on 24 September 1953 that I collected from the Companies Office in Pretoria the Memorandum, Articles and Certificate of Incorporation of Trek Airways (Proprietary) Limited – the birth of Trek. Jubilation was mixed, as far as I was

---

[1] 'Ou' is an Afrikaans word meaning 'fellow', referring to a male.

concerned, with trepidation – my faith in the chances of success of a charter company had been rudely shaken with Phoenix and the other eight airline casualties in recent years. But the die had been cast – make the most of it.

Trek's application for a charter licence to fly between South Africa and Europe was duly gazetted, and we decided to appoint an advocate to present our case to the National Transport Commission – we did not know the exact procedure. Although the minister had not yet released an aircraft, Fanie assured that this would in due course be done. Trek applied to have a DC-3 on its licence. The day of the application arrived and four of the Trek musketeers attended the hearing of the Commission. South African Airways naturally put in an objection and their counsel, Cecil Margo, spoke eloquently against the granting of our application. It was refused to our dejection.

The chairman of the NTC hearing was Brigadier Ross. During the war my auditing firm had been the regimental auditors of all messes and canteens in the Pretoria Headquarters Command area. During my frequent audits I had on many occasions been called to testify at courts martial, where Brigadier Ross was invariably in the chair, and we had become well acquainted. I therefore proposed to my fellow directors at Trek that I should privately approach the Brigadier and find out why our application had been rejected. It was only my close contact with the Brigadier that made this possible – it had to be off the record.

Brigadier Ross was a pleasant personality, with a large waxed handlebar moustache – an approachable man. He confidentially told me that there were two objections to our application. One, that we had no provision for adequate engineering facilities. Two, that we produced no evidence of having landing rights in Europe. This information gave us something to work on.

Engineering was a real problem – where to find someone to arrange an engineering set-up. Again Syd piped up – he had the answer. Tropic had a first-rate engineer in Fred Gratz. Syd arranged a meeting with the rather reluctant Gratz. Yes, he would like to help, but he was not prepared to jeopardise his position in Tropic Airways, where he was a key man, although not a director. It took a lot of persuasion from Syd, and not a little incentive from Fanie Botha, to make him agree to let his name go forward in a renewed application.

To arrange landing rights in Düsseldorf, Germany, was not difficult. Once more we made an application for a charter licence. It duly appeared in the *Government Gazette*. I talked my fellow musketeers into allowing me to appear for the hearing – I now knew the procedure. Also my many years as lecturer at Pretoria University in accounting as well as my long association as a Pretoria toastmaster with the Pretoria Toastmaster Club had given me confidence in public speaking. I had also done a certain amount of study in law.

I appeared and saved us the large fee charged by professional advocates. *Mirabile dictu* – Trek was awarded the licence. We were in business, but at that stage still without an aircraft. Eventually Fanie's minister came to light, but still there was another disappointment. He was only prepared to put up six hulls of DC-3s for auction. We had no option but to bid for one, which we acquired for £600.

It was at this stage that we at last had a lucky break. Tropic had folded up (voluntarily) and Fred Gratz was prepared to join Trek and convert the hull to an airworthy DC-3. Fred was now to become our engineering manager. Fanie's cheque for £15,000 went into our new bank account. Fred started to gather everything necessary for his conversion. Everything went well for the first few weeks at Rand Airport, where we had established an engineering workshop. Then Fred struck a snag (Trek always seemed to attract snags). There was no propeller shaft available for love or money. Work was held up for a few anxious weeks, until one day Fred announced that he had managed to get the necessary shaft from South African Airways.

And so it came about that Fred delivered a completely airworthy DC-3 on 15 December 1953. The next day, Dingaans Day (as it was then called), was a holiday, and was spent by all the directors and their wives at Rand Airport, working late into the night to complete the internal furnishings of the plane – curtains, mats, towels and so on. Near midnight work was finished, and the plane was ready for take-off early the very next morning with a full complement of passengers who had already booked their seats.

During the building up period Trek had made considerable progress in the set-up of the company's administration. When Syd reported to us the demise of Tropic, he immediately set up a meeting with Tom Meredith, a highly experienced and skilful pilot as well as being well-versed in operational requirements – we desperately needed an operational director. Tom was the man. None of us had met him until Syd introduced him to the three of us in an office in His Majesty's Building in Johannesburg, where we had acquired premises. As Tom was now at a loose end without Tropic, he jumped at the opportunity of again being in an airline, this time without Harry Creed. One stipulation he made was that his UK partner Jock Hamilton should also be brought into Trek – they would each contribute the initial amount of £1,000. Only Syd knew Jock, but he assured us that he was a good man to have, particularly as we would in any case need an overseas representative to initiate, regulate and control landing rights in various foreign countries. So Jock was in, and time was to prove what a valuable asset we had acquired in him. Jock became our overseas director, stationed in London. Tom joined us as operations manager. Rod Rooken-Smith decided to seek other pastures and we paid him out. In his place we introduced another pilot, Cecil Snelgar, who served the company faithfully for many years.

With all the preliminary negotiations Trek had not yet had a formal meeting to comply with the Companies Act – but this could wait; discussions were at this stage more important. During one of our first get-together discussions, Tom made an adamant point. In Tropic, he told us, one fundamental weakness lay in relying on travel agents for bookings. Tropic had employed an agent named Wally Thornhill, who had procured for them good loads of both passengers and freight. He was particularly good at arranging transport of gold to Europe for the mines. But he was equally good at holding Tropic to ransom for cut prices. If the cut was not big enough he would simply transfer the gold contract to a rival private operator flying from Lourenco Marques (as it was known in those days). So Tom was insistent that we must have our own commercial department to avoid such horse-trading.

He also had a suggestion for the man to organise and control the commercial department – General Helm von Mellenthin. Tom explained that he had met the General at parties of mutual friends, and was favourably impressed. Tom suggested to the General that if he would be willing to close his own travel agency, there would be an opening for him in Trek. We met the General ('Call me Helm'), were impressed, and made our offer to him to become Trek's commercial manager. He accepted readily, and was prepared to invest his £1,000 in Trek Airways (Pty) Ltd. He was appointed as commercial manager in July 1954.

Later, Jock told me that he had received three pleading letters from Tom during the early part of 1953 asking him to be one of the proposed shareholders in a new airline that was starting up. The proposal was that each one had to subscribe £1,000. Jock said that he had ignored the first two letters as the UK company seemed to have a promising future. However, at the time of Tom's third letter, Jock had decided to sell Gamsu to Davies and Newman (they had started 'Danair'). Jock said that he had sold them an aircraft from Gamsu. He then had £3,000. He transferred £2,000 to Tom in Johannesburg – £1,000 was to be Tom's share, the other £1,000 was his share. The remaining £1,000 was to be used to set up a London office. Jock told me that the amount he had actually received from Davies and Newman for Gamsu had been £18,500. In fact, Danair had done a good deal. It had fallen upon Jock to find a replacement aircraft. He had approached Airworks to buy a Viking that they had for sale. This was purchased for about £10,000 (Jock later bought two more for about the same price). The transaction was done with Air Safaris being the ostensible buyer. This company paid the monthly instalments to Lombard Bank.

The Trek directors in 1953 were:

William Buckland Rorke (Paddy), a chartered accountant practising in Pretoria, South Africa.

Cecil Snelgar, a pilot.

William Edward Hamilton (Jock), a former member of the RAF during the war years.

Tom Meredith, a former policeman in the UK. He joined the RAF in 1940.

- Rodney Rooken-Smith, a retired big game hunter from Kenya, Africa. When he resigned he was replaced with Cecil Snelgar.
- Fred Gratz, an aircraft engineer. During the war years he had joined the South African air force.
- Fanie Botha, a businessman and also the Mayor of Heidelberg in South Africa at the time.
- General Friederich Wilhelm von Mellenthin, a German who had been in the German cavalry, but during the war had been chief of staff in the Western Desert to Field Marshal Erwin Rommel, known as the 'Desert Fox'. He became a director in July 1954.

And, of course, Syd Excel, but owing to his criminal conviction, was not allowed to officially appear on the letterhead as a director of Trek. He was granted full director's rights and had full voting power in all Trek's board meetings.

At this stage let us have the background of the directors. Let us start with Fanie Botha.

Fanie Botha

It was in Heidelberg in South Africa that Fanie first saw the light of day. It was once described by a poet in South Africa in verse.

> *Ek wonder my steeds wat ons Dominee sou sê*
> *As die meisies by ons so min klere sou hê*
> *Maar gelukkig het hul 'n bietjie verstand*
> *Waar ou Heidelberg hang aan die Suikerbos Rand.*

An English bard might have expressed it as:

> I wonder myself what our churchman would say
> If our girls were to dress in nudist array
> But luckily for us they do understand
> Where old Heidelberg hangs on the Sugarbush Rand.

Yes, it was in this Heidelberg in the Transvaal that Fanie was bred, not in the Heidelberg of the Cape, or the one on the Rhine. From an early age Fanie Botha was a typical Afrikaner lad, fond of the outdoors and in love with the veld; quite at home with its wildlife, but rather to hunt than to preserve. At school he was bright enough, but in sport he revelled, especially in boxing. A heavyweight puncher he was certainly going to be, standing as he did at over six foot, which was the measure in those days.

In 1953 Fanie Botha was Mayor of Heidelberg in the Transvaal, South Africa, owner of two bottle stores and obviously well heeled. Fanie had brown wavy hair, broad shoulders and a friendly grinning face. He was extremely good-looking – as many young girls had experienced at some cost. According to Fanie, unless he ravished one or two maidens each week, the week was a write-off!

When the depression of 1930s South Africa hit, Fanie was engaged to Anne, also of Heidelberg, but suddenly he found himself unemployed. In desperation he made a pact with Anne. 'I am going to see the world for two years and make some money. After two years I shall return and marry you – you must wait for me!' So off Fanie went to Durban.

In Durban harbour Fanie managed to get appointed a stoker on a liner bound for New York. The tough job was no problem to one of his physique – at least he was working. Disembarking in New York he went in search of a job. First he had to have a decent meal.

As he walked the streets of Broadway with but a few coins in his pocket he noted the poverty and hunger all around. Then he learned that starvation was so prevalent that a statute had recently been passed making it illegal for any eating establishment to refuse food to anyone – but if at the end of the meal the diner could not pay, the house could employ chuckers-out who were entitled to assault the delinquent so as to dissuade him ever again to try for a free meal. But this only applied while the customer was still on the premises – if he could reach the pavement outside they could not touch him. Fanie decided on a free meal, and depended on his fists and feet to save him from the ejectors. He seated himself at a table where a ragged tramp was chancing his luck – he had not eaten for days, so the tramp's options were either dying or suffering a beating. So nervous was the tramp that he could barely lift his soup to his lips without spilling it. Fanie took pity on him. 'Don't worry old man, I will see that you are not beaten up. Trust me.' They finished the meal and the tramp even had a second course. Fanie explained his strategy. 'When the chucker-out arrives I am going to throw the table at him, and then we must run hell for leather for the door. Do not hesitate.' They both made the pavement, and had had a free eating session.

Fanie now felt better able to resume his walking up and down the streets of Broadway, Manhattan and even the West Side. All to no avail – there were no jobs. Then he had a stroke of luck – he met a recruiting officer for the gang of the notorious Al Capone, who was terrorising the whole of the States with his disdainful sidestepping of the draconian prohibition laws, rocking the American nation. Al Capone was all-powerful and even the FBI could not catch him out. The recruiter arranged a test to try and get Fanie accepted as a member of the gang. The pay was not bad, but the risk was considerable. Any gang member being caught might well face life imprisonment. But a man must eat.

Initiation into the gang was rigorous. One test was to be placed against a wall and have someone fire six revolver shots all around you – if you flinched, you were out. Then the positions were reversed and you had to fire the shots. If you hit your opponent, God help you!

Fanie was accepted to join the gang and stayed for some months. His job was on a ship bringing cargo into New York harbour – sacks of grain. His job also entailed slitting each sack and inserting a bottle of cheap whisky (remember that this was the time of prohibition). On arrival at the point, these sacks had to be carried down the gangway (this was also part of his job). He would then be met by a customs officer who would strike each sack with a large mallet, in search of any illicit liquor. If any bottle was found, the bearer would face a long term of imprisonment and all his co-sailors would also be arrested. It was not worth being caught out. However, one fine day, a bottle burst. Not waiting to see the outcome Fanie hastily dived overboard.

Eventually he landed up in Canada. But Al Capone shot fugitives from the gang, and so Fanie's life in Canada was a long nightmare. He was being tracked by Al Capone's men! Luckily he had befriended a young Canadian woman and he stayed locked up in her flat. When he realised that the flat was being watched by Al Capone's men, he decided his only solution to escape capture was to climb over the rooftops at night and get the hell out of Canada. Once more he made his way to the docks and managed to work his passage to Australia. He landed up in Sydney – penniless as usual. On the Sydney beach there were rows of prize-fighter boxing rings. This was the only way an ex-pro boxer could make a precarious living. You paid five pounds for three rounds against the ex-pro. If you lasted three rounds, you were paid ten pounds. However, if you knocked the ex-pro out, you were paid fifty pounds.

Fanie, being no mean boxer, borrowed five pounds from a local barman and started in the first ring. In all he fought in three rings and won each by a knockout – he had won £150. As he repaid his loan to the barman, he could not even drink a beer, as his face was a pulp, but at least he had money.

The only job available in Sydney was at the docks, this time as a loader of grain bags – but at least this was a legitimate cargo. Usually each bag required two men, but Fanie, being big and strong, carried a bag by himself and so earned two tokens instead of one. He soon learned to supplement his income by buying the supervisor a bottle of brandy in return for a handful of tokens – Fanie was always resourceful.

After a few weeks he was unloading a ship from South Africa and there he saw an old copy of *The Outspan* (in those days a well-known South African weekly). He devoured the news from South Africa but was shocked to see a picture of his Anne, now engaged to someone else. Fanie saw red! He jumped on the next boat and worked his passage back to his beloved South Africa, arriving on a Sunday in Heidelberg. Anne was in church with her new fiancé, but he dragged them both out, off to Anne's house. On arrival he ordered Anne to 'make some coffee' and as she left the room he tackled her unfortunate fiancé. 'Look here son, take back your ring from Anne and get the hell out of here, otherwise I'll knock your block off!' The fiancé made a hasty departure.

When Anne returned she said, 'Fanie, how could you! I have not heard a word from you for six months.' Said Fanie, 'Anne, don't be silly. I told you I was coming back to marry you – you know I never write. I still have one year to go and then we shall marry.'

All agreed, this time Fanie set off to England with the money he had made in Australia. Jobs in England were as scarce as blacks in the Broedersbond back in South Africa. In 1933 there were rumblings in Europe about the rise of a new dictator, Adolph Hitler. Winston Churchill's warnings were blatantly ignored, but nevertheless the Royal Navy put out a recruitment drive. In desperation Fanie enlisted and in due course found himself on a British cruiser at sea. Aboard was a shy and softly spoken man with a faint stutter. Fanie took pity on him, and was surprised to learn that he was a member of the British monarchy, by the name of Albert, better known as 'Bertie' – he was the Duke of York. Titles meant little to Fanie, but they struck up a friendship during the long cruise.

On the first shore leave Bertie invited Fanie to spend some time at his family home in Scotland. Fanie was surprised that the home turned out to be an elegant castle, and that Bertie was indeed a person of considerable status in Scotland, a royal prince and second in line to the British throne.

Fanie was basically a family man and often played with the two young children, Elizabeth and Margaret Rose. As he played with the Duke's two children, and often rocked the Princess Elizabeth on his knee, Fanie never for a moment dreamed that his shipmate was one day to become King George VI of England – and that the little playmate who was always so eager to hear about South Africa would later be Queen Elizabeth II. Fanie Botha's knowledge of South African politics, the veld and its myriad forms of wildlife and his general acumen in the affairs of business were vast and his interest was intense. But his knowledge of the British royal family was scant – frankly, like Clarke Gable, in *Gone with the Wind*, he 'didn't give a damn'. He enjoyed his jaunts with Albert to his Scottish home, and he developed an affection for his royal family. It is doubtful whether his confederates in the Broedersbond would have shared his sentiments – in fact I often used to wonder whether he ever disclosed to them his connection to the British royal family. I doubt it. But then our Fanie was a complex individual, a man of many parts.

After eighteen months Fanie returned to South Africa, married his Anne and they lived happily ever after, except that Fanie still had his passion for young women.

Fanie, in addition to his magnificent physique, had a shrewd and cunning business brain – also he was a man of many plans. In Rhodesia (as it was then) he built a large dam for the government, working day and night under floodlights. The government paid him an exorbitant sum for the dam, which was thereafter referred to as 'Huggins' Folly' (Huggins was the prime minister at the time).

Fanie was into any business venture where there was a quick profit and ended up with two valuable bottle stores. He then also became the mayor of Heidelberg. Politically he also knew which side his bread was buttered and he became second in command to the famous Broedersbond in the Transvaal. Fanie was a friend of the entire cabinet, on first-name terms with each succeeding prime minister – he was a man to be reckoned with. This was the Fanie that I was introduced to many decades ago in that cafe in Heidelberg. But more of Fanie later.

William Edward Hamilton (Jock), DSO, DFC

My first meeting with Jock Hamilton was impressive. When we had, somewhat hesitantly, allowed Tom Meredith to bring in Jock Hamilton as a shareholder, I had no idea what sort of character he was – Tom did not elaborate. We insisted that he fly from London to meet the board. I decided that we should welcome him with a company dinner at our house in Pretoria.

As the proposed directors for the new airline, Trek, and other important staff members sat with wives at five tables in our lounge, I rose for a speech of greeting for the man that I had only met for the first time that morning. As I was an experienced toastmaster I had no problem in giving a welcoming address of ten minutes. Applause and singing of 'For he's a jolly good fellow' followed. Jock sat immobile as a Buddhist deity, even as there were shouts of 'Speech!' Jock, seated next to me, whispered, 'What am I supposed to say?' I whispered back, 'Just stand up and say thank you.' Which is precisely what he did – two little words, not a syllable more! I mentally labelled him another taciturn Scot!

Only as the years went by did I come to know and to respect Jock as a man's man. A man of few words until roused – then a voluble man of action! It was many years after he joined Trek that I managed to drag from him memories of his earlier life.

His father, who was already fifty years of age when Jock entered the world on 2 April 1920, had had an adventurous existence. At the age of seventeen he had worked his passage from Scotland to South Africa, where he had worked in the Kimberly diamond mine until the Boer War started. He had then migrated to Canada, where he was employed as a subcontractor blasting rocks for the Canadian Pacific Railway. There he was reported killed in a rail crash, but in fact was only severely injured – he returned to his native Scotland and finished his career in a humdrum job with the London, Midland and Scottish Railway Company.

Jock, in his school days a mediocre and reluctant student, applied at the age of fourteen to join the RAF as a cadet. He was rejected because of a heart murmur. I still recall with admiration how at the outbreak of war he managed to pressure a recruiting officer into accepting him as an air-gunner and wireless operator – a pilot he could not be, as his murmur had persisted.

Jock had a proud war record. On his very first flight over enemy territory his crew flunked flying over the target area and dropped their bombs in the North Sea. It was one of those things that one never hears about in the heroic RAF – how often did it happen? Jock told his OC the very next morning that he refused to take off with that same crew ever again – he would not say why. He was transferred. As fate would have it, his old crew was wiped out over their target area on the next flight. Jock was lucky! His devotion to duty earned him a DFM (Distinguished Flying Medal).

After completing aircrew training he served in various capacities, mainly with the RCAF (Royal Canadian Air Force) on Whitleys, Wellingtons and Halifax aircraft, including one term as an instructor on a heavy conversion unit. His hankering after action prompted him to manage a transport command, where he met and crewed with flight officer Tom Meredith (in later life our own Captain Meredith).

Towards the end of the war in Europe Jock had a nerve-wracking experience. His bomber aircraft was badly shot away over Germany – the whole tail was open. Jock, with true Scottish determination, crawled to the gaping hole in the tail, mounted a puny machine gun and shot down two pursuing German fighters. It was this act of bravery that earned him his prestige decoration – the DFC – for courage of the highest order. Try as I could I never persuaded Jock to elaborate that epic episode – he was a truly taciturn Scot! The nearest I ever got was when he once just shrugged off my request for further details with a laconic 'I was lucky to be in the right place at the right time'. Modestly he did not add that he was also the right man.

In August 1946 he was asked by Tom Meredith to join him at Liverpool in a new company named Sky Travel – flying immigrants to South Africa in a Bristol Wayfarer. In August 1947 the company liquidated, leaving the two of them stranded in South Africa – babes in the wood! However, expenses were regularly sent by the liquidators which enabled them to live fairly comfortably in South Africa, helped every now and then by some freelance flying, until in February 1948 when they were required by the liquidators to fly the aircraft back to England. At last they were back in the UK.

Eventually they managed to join Pan African Air Charter Operation, flying mostly to Israel. This involved them in the first Israeli-Arab war, being indiscriminately shot at by both Israelis and Arabs. They were later sacked for refusing to cooperate in a currency racket in Geneva.

Next they managed to join Universal Air Transport, the forerunner of El-Al. There they met Fred Gratz and Cecil Snelgar who both later joined Trek. In between their ad hoc charter flights, Jock and Tom formed an air travel and aviation consultancy registered as 'Meredair'.

It was in 1950 that they met Harry Creed, who had acquired General Smuts' wartime plane. Together the three formed Tropic Airways with Harry Creed as managing director holding fifty per cent of the shares. Fred Gratz was given employment as chief engineer, and Sydney Excel flew ad hoc for Tropic from time to time.

In Tropic Airways Harry Creed was the great dictator, Tom and Jock were merely lackeys. Which was why they applied jointly to court for a judicial management order – based not on any difficulty of finance (of which there was none), but purely upon dispute between the directors. The order was granted, but naturally creditors foreclosed thinking that Tropic Airways was going insolvent. This friction between the directors ruined the company, whose bank account still showed a healthy balance.

As one studies the cut and thrust that went on between exwartime aviators desperately trying to become airline operators, one realises with a shudder what a tremendous hazard it was for those of us who were talked so glibly by Syd Excel into joining his madcap schemes, like that of forming a new charter airline to enable the public to holiday abroad to places they had heard of, but had never dreamed of seeing.

William Buckland Rorke (Paddy)

The career of William Buckland Rorke (Paddy) can conveniently be divided into several phases.

1915–1925: Van der Byl Street.

1926–1930: Pretoria Boys High School.

1931, the halcyon year: university.

1932–1938: slog and grind.

1939–1945: the war.

1945–1952: the professional period.

1953–1983: the rise of Trek/Luxavia.

1915–1925: Van der Byl Street

In the Transvaal (today's Gauteng) there nestled among developing coal fields a small *dorp* (village) called Witbank, some fifty miles east of Pretoria in South Africa. In 1915 my mother and father had left Pretoria as my father had got a job with the Transvaal and Delagoa Bay mine (T and DB) in a clerical position.

I was born on 22 February 1915 – there had only been one white birth in Witbank that day. Believe it or not, I weighed twelve pounds. I was registered with the family names: William Buckland.

My first years on earth remain very hazy. My father was Claude Oriel Rorke and my mother was Kathleen Elizabeth Jeanette Rocher. In Witbank I also had at that time a bachelor brother of my father, Uncle Jim, whom I do not remember because he sadly passed away in a railway coach from a sudden heart attack – this shortly after my arrival. But it was Uncle Jim who gazed at my cot on that great day and exclaimed, 'Still, this is not the girl that we all expected? I know what I shall call him – Paddy, the next best thing.' And so 'Paddy' has stuck to me throughout my life. No one has ever dared call me William. The sad demise of Uncle Jim, so soon after, hit my father very badly. It was then that he decided to call me by the nickname of 'Jim'. I never once heard him call me Paddy, but everyone else did. With Dad's penchant for nicknames he always called my mother 'Pat' – but never would he explain why. It must have been his distorted Irish sense of humour, which bubbled out of him throughout his life – a likeable and well-loved man.

So we became a trio – Claude, Pat and Paddy.

My father was born in Somerset East, South Africa, of a father who came from County Cork in Ireland to join the 1820 settlers in the Eastern Province. My grandfather was William Benjamin Rorke, who passed away before my arrival. He had two other brothers who had also left Ireland. The family name had originally been O'Rourke, but on arrival in South Africa they had decided to change it to plain Rorke. My one uncle started a trading store near Ladysmith – Rorke's Drift – where the British and Zulus had a bloody encounter. My grandmother visited us once in Pretoria before she too passed on.

Shortly after my birth my father enlisted in the South African contingent to thwart the German forces in German South West Africa. The 1914–1918 war had begun. My mother moved to Cape Town and we set up home with my father's sister, Ella Buckland.

I was three years old when I set eyes on my father for the first time. My father decided to settle in Pretoria where he was fortunate to find secretarial employment with the railways, the Zuid-Afrikaanse Spoorwegen, near to the main Pretoria Railway Station.

In 1921 my brother Bryan was born. My father never had a nickname for Bryan but I called him 'the bantam dawdler' because being so much younger and smaller than me, he could not keep up with me. The following year I started school. My school years were spent by normal standards – only eight years (six to fourteen). I was not the brightest boy in the class, but I seemed to have acquired the knack of satisfying the teachers without devoting too much time to my studies. I was more interested in sport.

1926–1930: Pretoria Boys High School

My secondary education was spent at Pretoria Boys High School. It was there that I found that I enjoyed sport. I captained the prestigious under-fourteen teams at both cricket and rugby, but was too young and inexperienced to earn more than a second team cap. Although I occasionally played for the first XI. In under-fourteen cricket, I established a school record against St John's College in Johannesburg by scoring 112 not out before lunch. On leaving school I offered a complete outfit to anyone breaking the record. This stood for twenty-five years and was curiously enough broken by a son of one of the members of the under-fourteen side who played on the day when I had established the record. Quite a coincidence! I also held the 880 yard under-fifteen record for about twenty years (time only 2.15.2 minutes).

1931, the Halcyon Year: University

On matriculating I was still undecided about a career and so my father sent me to Rhodes University, making 1931 a really happy year for me. But then the worldwide depression struck and I was forced to return to Pretoria and go out to work – my father lost his job. It was decided that I should become articled to the worldwide firm of accountants, Price Waterhouse.

1932–1938: Slog and Grind

I finished my B.Com degree at Pretoria University extramurally in 1933 and qualified as a chartered accountant in 1936. Unfortunately, my father died suddenly of a heart attack three months before I qualified. His estate was ravished by the depression, so he only left £400 and no house. We had no income and my brother, six years younger than me, still had three years of schooling to do. Times were tough!

After qualifying, I had to find a job. I was lucky to be appointed secretary to Beckett and Murray, a department store. They were cautious about employing me as I was only twenty-one and had to control an office staff of eight women. But I managed. My salary was a princely sum of twenty-seven pounds and ten shillings per month. This as a qualified CA – but times were hard.

At this time, Pretoria University was switching to entirely Afrikaans tuition and was having difficulty finding an accounting lecturer who could cope with Afrikaans – there were few Afrikaans textbooks on accounting. They required someone who could lecture in Afrikaans and who was in practice as an accountant. It was essential that the applicant also held an academic degree. I was the only one in Pretoria with these qualifications. Thus I was appointed. My Afrikaans was not very good and I had never studied accounting in Afrikaans. But I needed the job. They thought I was a bit too young to cope with extramural students, who were usually well into their twenties, but I said, 'Give me a try.' Furthermore, Dr Arndt (who was the dean at this time) had just published a new English/Afrikaans Commercial Dictionary. I said, 'If you appoint me I will insist that every student buys your dictionary as it would assist them with their studies.' Needless to say, I got the job. My lecture hours were Mondays and Wednesdays, 5–6.30 p.m. and 8–9.30 p.m.

I also took a job at Pretoria Technical College (at one pound and one shilling per hour). Over the weekends I rewrote the accounting lectures for the University Correspondence College and marked their students' papers (the fee was six pence per question). This way our family survived and my brother matriculated also at Pretoria Boys High School. In 1936, I started my own practice as an auditor.

An old school friend of mine, Brian Gibson, at that time was in partnership with an elderly CA who had been about for many years. Their firm was appointed official auditors of all military messes and canteens in the Transvaal. As war clouds were gathering in Europe during 1939, their burden of work became too great and I had been helping them two to three days each week. When it was announced that Italy had come into the war, Gibson and I were auditing at Defence Headquarters. The brigadier in charge asked us to consider enlisting as supervisors of messes and canteens with the rank of a captain. Unfortunately, the OC only required one of us. So Brian and I decided to toss a coin. He won and joined up. Brian's old partner was furious that Brian had abandoned him and summarily dismissed him, while offering me Brian's job. I agreed to take Brian's place, provided that he took Brian back into the firm on full pay throughout the war. This he did, provided I gave an undertaking not to join up. He said the military needed our services as accountants! Later Brian transferred to the air force.

1939–1945: The War

So this was how I spent much of the wartime years in military messes and canteens, often sleeping in military camps, but never in uniform. This was a bit hard to bear, enduring years of jibes, but I had given my word not to enlist. I survived and so did Brian, who returned to Pretoria after peace was declared in 1945. Throughout the war I constantly had to work long hours to cope with the audits – usually up to 9 p.m. or 10 p.m., Mondays to Fridays. I kept on lecturing at the university. I only retired from that post after twenty-seven years.

1945–1952: The Professional Period

In 1945 I married Ticatic, an old flame of mine, who had just become divorced and settled down to a new life. I managed to build up my finances reasonably. However, I indulged in promoting many types of enterprises as well as running my accountancy practice, which was flourishing. These sidelines that I was involved in were two ladies' hairdressing salons, Economic Dairies, developing a township (Tileba), a window-model factory and a slate quarry. I even financed a pop star group. Most of these ventures cost me dearly. And then in 1953 came Trek Airways.

1953–1983: The Rise of Trek/Luxavia

I still retained my auditing practice but I went headlong into Trek. These were extremely interesting years and very rewarding in many respects.

Our Trek board met every Friday in Johannesburg (our business base) from 9 a.m. usually up to 5 or 6 p.m. This was a fascinating time, and as chairman and also financial director of Trek, I travelled the world, usually three or four times a year to England and the continent. We had offices in Düsseldorf, Hamburg, Luxembourg, Amsterdam and London. My particular beat was Liechtenstein where we had managed to negotiate a twenty-year tax agreement with their government. My one real disappointment was when the board refused to ratify my agreement with John Foggitt of TFC Tours. Through this stupidity, Trek threw away an income of many millions over the years. However, I personally had many happy hours with John Foggitt and he was always grateful for my efforts to involve Trek in his tours. John gave me many complimentary tickets to the East (Bangkok, Hong Kong and Japan), as well as cruises to the Seychelles, Mauritius and around the Greek islands. What a wonderful time it was – never to be forgotten, and making so many good friends throughout the world. Icelandic Airways offered me a free flight to America and the Bahamas with a full day in Iceland, where my wife and myself were shown much of Iceland and royally entertained.

It often happened that our Trek flights were so full (our average load factor was 95–98%), that I often had to apply to SAA, who at all times were prepared to give me a complimentary first-class flight. What a pity it all had to come to an end after twenty-five years – but what memories!

Sydney Excel

Syd was, from his earliest years, self-opinionated and always most self-assertive; this attitude at school created many enemies and not a few fights. However at sport he was often a hero, particularly in the swimming world. He left school at the first opportunity, and ran away to become a mercenary in General Franco's revolution, where he learned to use weapons.

He only arrived at the tail end of the war, and then came back home. His father was in a quandary as to what to do with his errant son, and so forced him into the South African Police – no doubt hoping that the military training would settle him down. What a hope! September 1939 found Syd eagerly following Hitler's indiscretions. When war was declared Syd was ecstatic. No longer the drudgery of police investigation for him. To battle! Unfortunately, the police authorities refused to release him to join the air force (his heart's desire), and so he had no option but to enlist with the Police Corps together with hundreds of his co-trainees. Syd was unhappy and kept applying for transfer to the air force, without success. When the first month's military pay was received there was a general grumble – they had been docked mess fees of two shillings per day, which gave them less income than they had received before enlisting. Syd became their self-appointed leader and proved to be a real rabble-rouser. He led the whole contingent on a sit-down strike – no one went on parade. The usual army punishment was ineffective due to the large number of dissenters.

The OC decided in an inspirational flash that the quickest solution was to get rid of Private Excel. Syd was transferred immediately to the Western Desert – but still with the Police Corps, now an armed car division.

Syd began once again with his agitation for transfer to the air force. His OC in the desert was not without information about Excel's conduct down south, and promptly blue-pencilled his name from the monthly transfer lists. After a few months Syd became despondent and so reverted to type – he staged a one-man sit-down strike. He refused to go on parade and went on a starvation diet. His superbly fit physical condition made such a strike a feasible proposition, and he survived weeks of CB ('confined to barracks').

The OC had more serious matters to occupy him than Private Sydney Excel and shelved his responsibility by sending the culprit back south to Weskoppies Asylum in Pretoria for mental observation. Back home in Pretoria in the institution, Syd resumed normal eating habits and strove to build up his physical condition by exercising sessions.

This had its results as Syd managed to persuade the tribunal appointed to look into his case with his glib tongue and fervour, that he was perfectly sane, and only wanted to fly for the war effort. Mirabile dictu! They granted his request and in due course Syd got his wings – triumph for perseverance.

Through the war Syd flew both in the Union and up north in transport aircraft. He was never made a fighter pilot, but flew many sorties without any conspicuous achievements. After the armistice he stayed on for a considerable period, carrying out various transportation chores.

Finally demobilisation came – what to do next? He was certainly not going back to the police. As a temporary measure he joined in the conduct of shooting safaris. This gave him plenty of time to dream up his future. This is when he approached me and involved me in his future enterprises – African Air Safaris, Phoenix Airlines and finally his brainchild which became known as Trek!

Tom Meredith

Tom was born in a small English town of Bilston in May 1912. He was one of nine children. In 1936, he was accepted as a cadet officer in the Liverpool City Police. He stayed with the force for five years. When war broke out in 1939, Tom was a constable. In 1941 the War Office started recruiting as many men as possible and, at last, Tom's dream of becoming a pilot materialised. He was accepted into the Royal Air Force and was sent for initial training at Stratford-upon-Avon. In early 1942 he obtained his wings. At last he was a pilot in the RAF. It was in the RAF that he met Jock Hamilton, and after the war, in 1946, Tom and Jock formed a company called Sky Travel to fly immigrants to South Africa. This was not a great success, but it paved the way for further ventures. Tom and Jock then became involved with Pan African Air Charter.

In 1948, Tom and Jock formed an air travel and aviation consultancy known as Meredith and Hamilton. Later, in association with Harry Creed, the three of them bought General Smuts' old Avro York and operated a passenger service to Europe under the name of Tropic Airways. This company operated very successfully until it was broken up by the disagreement between the three shareholders, already mentioned. With this discord Tropic Airways folded up. Tom in the meantime became aware of the formation of a new company in South Africa, to be called Trek.

Tom died in January 2000 in Johannesburg, South Africa.

Fred Gratz

Fred served with SAAF during the war. A technical man with a very sound knowledge of aircraft engineering technique, he was a good businessman, an exceptionally hard and efficient worker. Syd Excel had always been very impressed with him.

It so happened that when Trek purchased the DC-3 hull from the air force in 1953, Fred was invited to join the team. He established a workshop and with the staff he employed he made it possible to deliver a beautiful and highly efficient passenger DC-3 aircraft in less than six months.

Throughout his association with Trek and Luxavia, he provided high quality aircraft engineering and was always a kingpin in maintaining Trek's efficiency.

Cecil Snelgar

Cecil was born 23 May 1913 in Grahamstown. He became a manufacturing chemist for Kowie Medicine (Pty) Ltd. He played rugby for Border before the war, and was invited to participate in the Springbrook rugby trials, though, unfortunately, he was not chosen. He joined the SAAF during the war years and flew from 1940–1946. From 1947–1949, he flew as a pilot for Suidar International Airline, and then from 1949–1953 for Union of Burma. Then he was a pilot and a director for Trek Airways.

General Helm von Mellenthin

General Helm von Mellenthin was born in Prussia on 30 August 1904. After leaving school he enlisted in the German cavalry, where he spent many happy and successful years. He had an innate love of horses and was a champion in the field of dressage. By 1939 he had achieved prestige in the military hierarchy. It was no surprise when he was transferred to the North African Campaign, in the prize position of Rommel's chief of staff in the Western Desert. He was fortunate to survive Rommel's later defeats, and to come through hostilities unscathed. Before the war he had married a charming German girl, Inge, and they had produced a son, Friedrich (Friewi).

After the armistice Inge persuaded Helm to start a new life in South Africa where she had relatives. Between them they established a travel agency in Johannesburg – German South African Airlines. The war was still too much in the memories of people to make them keen to patronise a German-operated concern, and the new business only showed meagre results. Tom Meredith had met the von Mellenthins at parties of mutual friends, and was favourably impressed. The General eventually became commercial manager of Trek and invested £1,000 in Trek Airways (Pty) Ltd.

Thus when the Trek shareholders assembled at Rand Airport on that joyous day of 15 December 1953, the company had overnight been transformed into a United Nations concern – one Englishman, one Scot, one German, one Kenyan, three South Africans and one dyed-in-the-wool Broederbonder. Quite a goulash. But somehow it worked.

He died in Johannesburg in 1996, at the age of ninety-two.

Board Rumblings

Our first flight was off and safely back, with full complements of pax each way, future bookings were starting to roll into our new commercial booking office in His Majesty's Building in the Johannesburg CBD and so the time had come to forget our Christmas festivities and to comply with the requirements of the Companies Act. We summoned our first official board meeting.

As 1954 dawned, our shareholders gathered for the first actual business proceeding. Naturally Fanie Botha was elected to the chair and appointed managing director (in today's terms, CEO). Then one by one the directors were voted upon and appointed. Tom Meredith, General Helm von Mellenthin, Jock Hamilton and myself. Rod Rooken-Smith was not interested in being a director, or for that matter in being involved with the day-to-day running of the company. He just wanted to get back to East London. When the elections closed Syd Excel piped up, 'What about me?' I explained to him, as I had previously done, that he was ineligible to be appointed a director as he had a criminal conviction for shooting at Elliot Wilson. I told him that we had all agreed that although he could not be registered as a director at this stage we would still regard him as one, with all the full rights and privileges, and at board meetings he would have the same vote as anyone else. It was still too soon after his conviction to apply to the Minister of Economic Affairs to have directorship status restored to him. But in time it would be done. Syd blew his top. 'I demand that my name go on the letterheads now.' I reiterated my words and explained that at present we could not describe him as a director – but to give it time. He stormed out of the room shouting, 'You're a two-faced lot of bastards.' As he shut the door he exclaimed, 'I'll teach you buggers.' He was gone. 'He'll get over his tantrum,' I assured the others. But I was wrong.

That evening, as I sat at home in Pretoria, he came to visit. But this time it was no social call. He was fuming. He then pulled a revolver out of his pocket and laid it on the table in front of him. 'You have double-crossed me,' he shouted and adopted a menacing attitude. I tried not to show that I was afraid of what he might do in his state of hysteria – with Syd you never knew what he was capable of. It took me half an hour to quiet him down, and he stormed out with another veiled threat. I did not sleep well that night – I was genuinely sorry for the man who had brought us so far in Trek, a company that now promised a great future. Ah well!

Within a few days the basis of Syd's threats emerged. Fred Gratz was arrested for the theft of a propeller shaft from South African Airways, based upon a statement from Sydney Excel. It was some months before Fred appeared in court and had to plead guilty. In mitigation he stated that the shaft was essential to Trek to avoid loss of jobs to the employees, and big financial loss to the company. Furthermore he had offered to pay for the spare but his mate in SAA said that this was impossible as it had been taken unofficially. Fred was convicted and Trek had to pay a substantial fine. Fred was also barred from the directorate of the company. He never went onto the board, but still attended all meetings and voted as an ordinary director – just as Syd would have done had he not lost his cool.

Naturally after Syd's perfidy, we could no longer keep him at Trek – so the man who had dreamed up, persistently pushed for and eventually brought to fruition our airline was the first to leave. We took back his shares for £1,000, gave him a Trek night-stop bag with two complimentary tickets to Europe and thanked him for what he had achieved, while wishing him well in the future.

The first of our four original musketeers was gone. I was sad to see him go – we owed him so much. No Syd – no Trek.

Flight Schedules and Service

After the Excel hiccup all departments of Trek settled down to get on with the task of providing the public with safe flying, good catering on board, enjoyable and interesting night-stops and reliability of take-off and landing times. Our licence only permitted us fifty-two flights per year. Although a charter licence is not supposed to work to a regular schedule, we took off every week from Jan Smuts Airport at 6 a.m. on a Friday and took four days to reach our destination, with three overnight stops. It was Fred Gratz's task to see that there were no undue delays in take-offs, no hazards while in the air and safe landings. This he achieved perfectly by organising a highly efficient engineering set-up. During the whole of the forty years' existence of Trek, not a single accident spoilt our record, not a passenger injured. Only once was there an emergency landing in the desert, which we knew was due to sabotage against South Africa. All pax returned safely. Such was Fred's efficiency.

Tom Meredith in his department was responsible for providing reliable and customer-friendly crews, and of course excellent hotels en route – only the best five-star hotels where possible. This he achieved with the distinction that made Trek flights so popular with air travellers of all classes – holiday as well as business. Our seat utilisation was probably a world record for flights of great distance. Annually it was consistently close to 100% over a year – well into the 90s. Our credo was that the customer always came before profit. Our advertising budgets were cut to the bone; rather we spent the saving on making our flight services so outstanding that word of mouth became our main advertisement. It worked. Even today, so many years since our last flight, many seasoned travellers talk with nostalgia about the good old days of Trek – why were jets ever invented!

Night flying with Trek was taboo – except in emergencies, which there hardly ever were. Take-offs from all stopovers were at 6 a.m., just in time for a good but very early breakfast. The first stop after take-off from Jan Smuts was for refuelling at perhaps Lusaka, then on to Entebbe, landing at about 5 p.m. The pax were invariably thrilled with the excellent hotel on the banks of the great lake of Victoria, almost on the equator. Short bus tours were usually arranged to show them the terrain, the lush tropical vegetation and the general countryside. Should Lake Victoria Hotel be booked out during the season, they would be taken to nearby Kampala. This also appealed to the travellers as it gave an insight into tropical Africa. The hotel was unusual, with no air conditioning, but overhead fans in all bedrooms. It certainly conveyed an African atmosphere.

All aboard at 6 a.m., on to Khartoum slap bang in the middle of the African desert – but only to refuel. Then hours over the great Sahara Desert, awakening memories for many of the North African campaign with Tobruk and Rommel. Nostalgic – especially when General von Mellenthin was aboard. He entertained me once for hours pointing out landmarks of interest, memories of wartime battles, still pinpointed by numerous wrecks of tanks and aircraft lost in the heat of raids of either General Montgomery or perhaps General Rommel.

And so to Cairo where the famous Shepherds Hotel of wartime fame had been superseded by the magnificent Nile Hilton Hotel – pure luxury. Naturally, as soon as possible after arrival at 5 p.m. excursions would be laid on for the pax to see the Sphinx and Pyramids. Opposite the Nile Hilton Hotel was one of Cairo's most exclusive markets, the Ding Dong Bazaar. By arrangement with its manager, our pax would be dropped off right in front of this vast shopping bazaar. In return for this favour the manager would insist on entertaining me in his luxurious but very Arabic office at the back of the bazaar. I soon learned not to refuse his offer of a *kleine-kleine*, which was always the same mixture – a Cypriot brandy followed instantly by a Hellenic beer to douse the inner burning. Ugh!

But I dared not refuse and had to talk to avoid a second dose of the same medicine. I wonder if the local Arabs really liked such a concoction. The brave front which I was forced to put on was, however, always rewarded by the parting gift of an attractive

Egyptian camel saddle. My Pretoria home built up quite a stock of camel saddles – they made good gifts for Christmases or weddings.

Should Cairo be crowded out, Trek would be forced to book in at Luxor situated near the world-renowned Valley of the Kings. A delicious foretaste for the pax of the wonder of ancient Egyptian mythology, history and culture. An unforgettable experience. Not a modern five-star hotel like the Nile Hilton, but a gracious Tudor-style hotel as only found in olde England. But it was comfortable, with an excellent table and service. In its way it was an experience as unforgettable as the Sphinx and the Pyramids. It likewise thrilled the pax.

At daybreak we would set off again, bound for Europe. The refuelling would be done on the northernmost tip of Africa, on the banks of the Mediterranean, possibly Wadi Haifa. Suddenly the vast, waste expanse of the Western Desert would be magically replaced by the blue expanse of the picturesque Mediterranean – a breathtaking contrast. Once out of Africa, there would be a variety of selected night-stops, depending on the seasonable influx of tourists around the popular seaside holiday resorts. Sometimes Trek would use Malta – in fact, whenever this was possible. The George Cross Island was of much interest, not only for its brave resistance during the war, but also for its famous labyrinth of caves, its rugged rocky coastline and its universally-admired lace industry. The Phoenicia Hotel too, was a Mecca for sun-searching trippers, relaxing in luxury in the warm heat and enjoying the attraction of exciting menus, exotic wines and courteous service. This island was an experience almost overlooked by South African tourists abroad – it was really a bonus offered by Trek.

Alternative third night-stops varied from Palma, Majorca, Nice, Barcelona and even as far afield as Vienna. It was in Vienna on a stopover that I bumped into Mimi Coertse many years ago when she was making her debut in the Vienna Staatsopera. She invited me to meet her pianist friend Dawid Engela in her attic flat, where they both entertained me to an evening of singing. She also engineered me a ticket to her opening night in the Opera House – only standing room at the back of the theatre, but I enjoyed it.

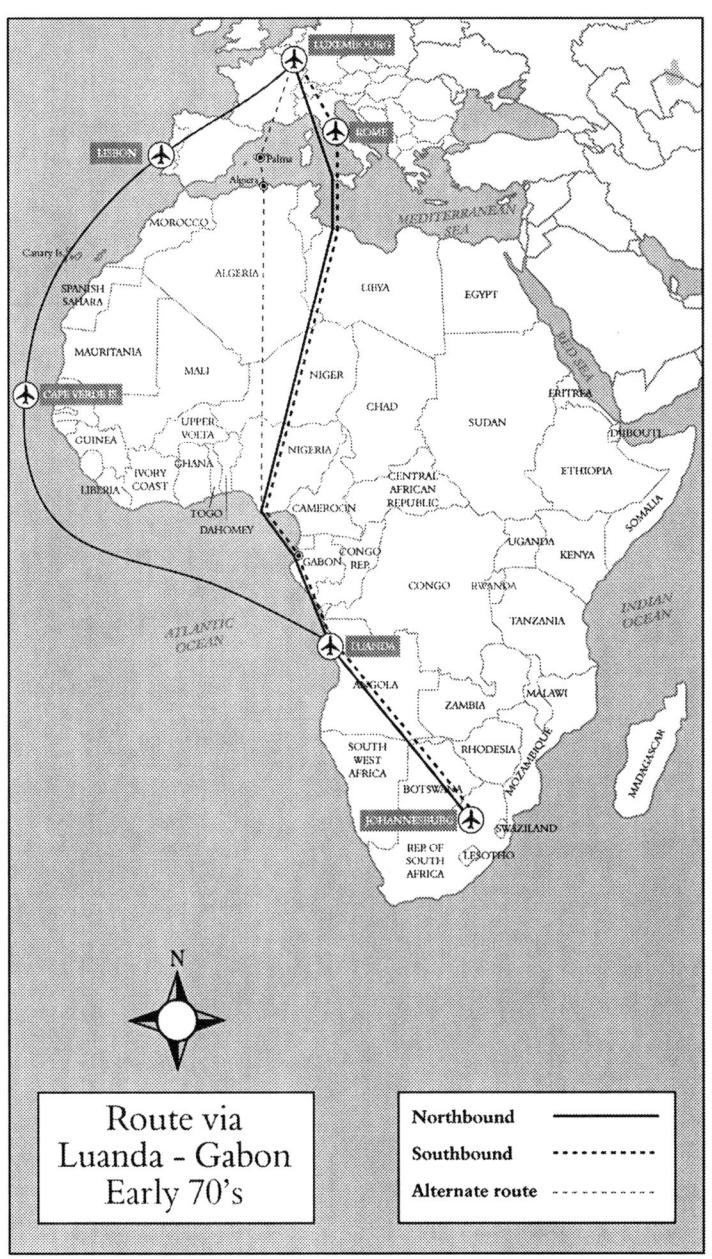

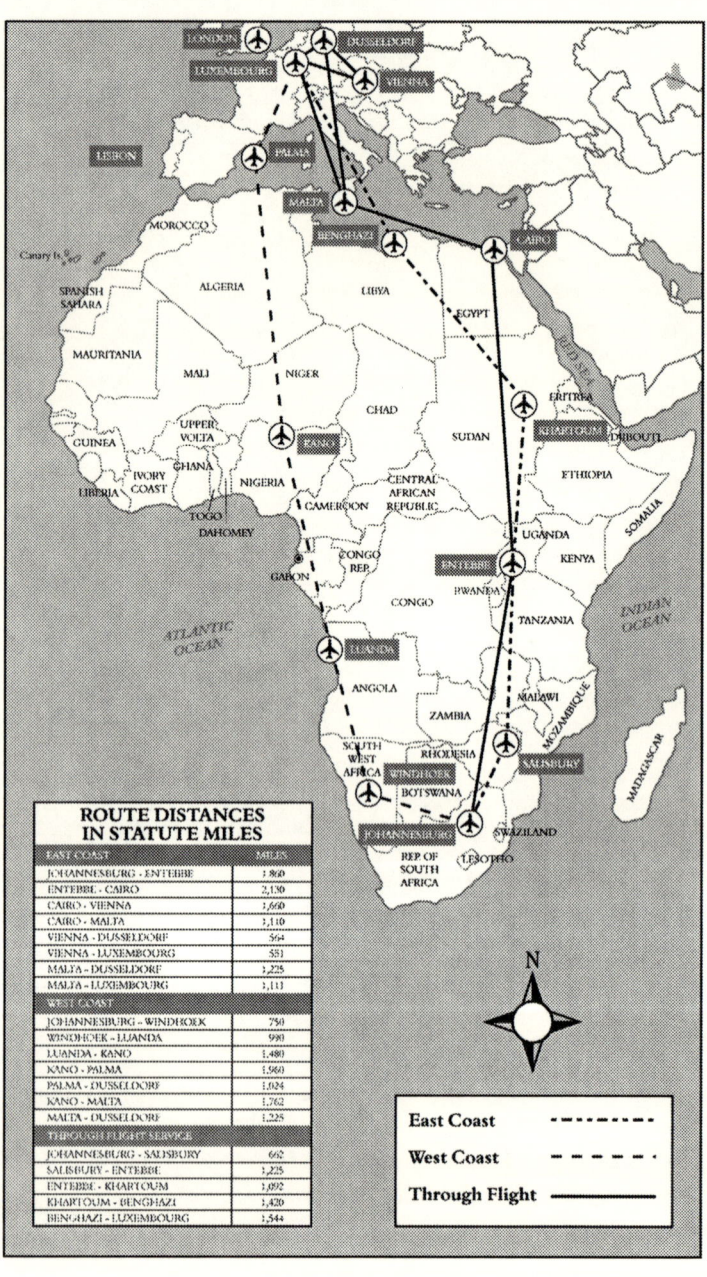

ROUTE DISTANCES IN STATUTE MILES

EAST COAST	MILES
JOHANNESBURG - ENTEBBE	1,860
ENTEBBE - CAIRO	2,130
CAIRO - VIENNA	1,660
CAIRO - MALTA	1,110
VIENNA - DUSSELDORF	564
VIENNA - LUXEMBOURG	551
MALTA - DUSSELDORF	1,225
MALTA - LUXEMBOURG	1,113
WEST COAST	
JOHANNESBURG - WINDHOEK	750
WINDHOEK - LUANDA	990
LUANDA - KANO	1,480
KANO - PALMA	1,960
PALMA - DUSSELDORF	1,024
KANO - MALTA	1,762
MALTA - DUSSELDORF	1,225
THROUGH FLIGHT SERVICE	
JOHANNESBURG - SALISBURY	662
SALISBURY - ENTEBBE	1,225
ENTEBBE - KHARTOUM	1,092
KHARTOUM - BENGHAZI	1,420
BENGHAZI - LUXEMBOURG	1,544

East Coast ·–·–·–·
West Coast – – – –
Through Flight ———

The final leg of our trip would terminate in any one of our original landing rights – usually Düsseldorf, but also possibly Paris, Amsterdam, Hamburg or even Southend in England. Alas, as time moved on and apartheid caught up with us, these termini were closed to us, one by one, until only Luxembourg remained. But while it lasted the variety added spice to the flight, and attracted as many pax as we could comfortably handle.

Our on-board meals were always the best that various local caterers could offer; all drinks during the flight were on the house, but not overdone; all tours and excursions were at no cost to the pax. I recall one occasion when General von Mellenthin insisted that we should serve caviar with the lunch meal. I happened to be on the trial flight, and saw that almost all the expensive caviar was returned uneaten to the galley. Then the penny dropped. The pax did not know what the little black balls were! Before the next meal the captain announced that caviar would now be served. At this announcement there was applause and every plate was returned completely empty – everyone was very impressed. The experiment did not last long as the cost was prohibitive, but it was good advertising value.

During flights Trek tried to give the pax something for their money. Should the crew spot anything of particular interest on the ground, perhaps a waterfall, a large herd of African animals or even a volcano such as Etna, the captain would descend from the usual 8,000-feet altitude to possibly 200 feet and would circle so that everyone could get a glimpse of the phenomenon. Furthermore, if favourable tailwinds should bring us early to Jan Smuts Airport, he would circle the East or West Rand so as to arrive spot on time. People waiting at the airport to meet Trek passengers would appreciate this consideration. Pax hate to arrive before the advertised ETA, which was another Trek service. The running of the entire Trek organisation was always customer-related. We wanted a good name above huge dividends. It paid off.

Administration

Within the first six months our organisation of the company's administration had settled down, and the various departments were running well. Fred's engineering workshop encountered few difficulties, and those that were experienced were efficiently handled by him. We had no problem with the operation of the DC-3, few delays and a 100% safety record. Syd had not exaggerated when he described Fred as a genius.

Helm's commercial section was organised with typical Germanic thoroughness, and advance bookings were above expectations. Tom's flights always left on time, and passenger reactions were excellent. Trek was quickly building a good reputation – travellers were starting to talk – our service was paying off. Jock's weekly reports were always to the point, sometimes too much to the point, occasionally vitriolic, but always prepared in the best interests of the company. We did not take exception to them, but did not blindly follow his frequent recommendations. In the early days when Trek had many options for termini, Jock kept in good touch with the aviation authorities at the various landing grounds. Trek's image was being built up as a reliable airline in Europe, thanks to Jock's cooperation with them.

Only in one department did we have a headache, a very big headache – in my section, finance. The South African revenue authorities had some years previously amended the Income Tax Act to the effect that income was taken to be not only the profit as shown by the annual financial statements, but in addition any moneys received in advance, for example, deposits. This was of course against all accounting principles, and it still pertains to this very day. It was a heinous enactment, which could stifle any business. In my practice I had an example where a newly established concern was forced to close its doors because of this clause. It concerned an ambitious man who set up a company to assist householders. A property owner could sign a contract with this man's firm to pay a monthly deposit, in return for which the company undertook to repair all electrical, plumbing or other ordinary maintenance shortcomings, free of charge – the monthly deposit was actually an insurance against such property defects. The idea appealed to many householders. But when I pointed out that the company would be taxed on the amount of deposits received even before any income was made, the company could not afford the taxation in advance of income – very unfair. But when I pointed this out to our local receiver of Revenue his bland comment was, 'Surely you do not expect income tax to be fair, Mr Rorke.' Nuff said!

Trek received many thousands of pounds (in those days) in deposits, even running to over a million pounds. To have to pay tax on these amounts even before the flights were due to take off would have put us out of business immediately. The receiver refused to allow us any relief. The law was the law. What to do?

At this stage I should mention that when I agreed to come into Syd's Trek Airways I made two stipulations. One, that I should be a director. Two, that regular meetings of the board must be held each week, and that at such occasions each director must present a weekly report. The air was too volatile not to be constantly supervised. This plan we adhered to strictly every Friday from 9 a.m. usually to 5 p.m. How many business concerns kept such a tight rein on their proceedings? It paid off – each section cooperated with the others to ensure a smooth-running, well-controlled enterprise. This is what made Trek so efficient over so many years.

It was at one of our first Friday board meetings that I posed my problem. The others merely shrugged it off – 'That's your department. Fix it up mate.' They neither understood nor cared about my dilemma. Each director had his own worries in his own department. He had to bring them before the board, but it was his duty to find the solution, fix it up and report back at the next meeting.

There was only one solution for me – to take advance fares out of the books of Trek. But how to do this? All such moneys would have to be paid to an outside agent, who would hold them safely until they were required for the particular flight. Where could we find a reliable agent with whom to entrust amounts running into seven figures? Obviously we had to control such an agent and the location had to be outside South Africa – far from the rapacious fingers of the SA Revenue Service. I scoured the usual overseas tax havens – Panama, the Channel Islands, Switzerland, Luxembourg and so on. Eventually I hit on Liechtenstein. It was isolated, but still conveniently close to our main European office in Düsseldorf. I had to study an atlas to find where Liechtenstein was situated – I found it eventually lying with Italy in the south, Germany in the north and Switzerland to the west.

We had put General von Mellenthin's son, Friewi, in charge of our Düsseldorf office. I asked him to investigate Liechtenstein to try to find a reliable firm there with whom we could negotiate. With the same Germanic efficiency as his father, Friewi reported back that he had arranged with a Dr O Tundury in Vaduz.

It was in search of Liechtenstein that Friewi and I went in May 1954. Our meeting in Vaduz was only in three days' time, so we took our time to meander down the Rhine on a glorious summer's day – hot, but perfect. It was my first glimpse of the German countryside, and the Rhine is a beautiful river, full of barge activity and with old castles visible, set in the typical German woodlands with the occasional deer. We appreciated Hitler's Autobahns, and spent two nights in B&B accommodation in small villages off the beaten track. For me it was more of a holiday than a business trip. But the important part started when we met Dr Otto Tundury in Vaduz. He was an erect, fairly thickset man originally from Switzerland. Like most Swiss he was at first rather distant, aloof – not a hail-fellow-well-met type. It was to take at least four years with visits twice per year before he asked me to call him Otto, and invited me to his lovely home to meet his charming wife and two well-mannered children, a boy and a girl. After that I was always welcomed by his family, and my wife became good friends with them. Years later my wife and I were sad to receive a funeral notice from Otto announcing that his teenage son had been killed in a skiing accident.

Dr Tundury was a lawyer by profession, but now conducted a business catering for overseas concerns who had tax problems.

That was just what we had come for. He advised us to register an *Anstalt* (much akin to our present-day CC in South Africa). He would be sole director, and no Trek names would appear anywhere. He would be directly responsible to Trek's board. As far as income tax in Liechtenstein was concerned, he undertook to make a suitable agreement with the local tax authority. This he very successfully did – the *Anstalt* would for twenty years have a tax agreement to pay a fixed income tax of 400 Swiss francs per annum, irrespective of profits or receipts. This is precisely what Trek wanted. We agreed that the name would be Luftverkeers Anstalt, and I insisted that the Memorandum and Articles of Association be drawn up in German, as far removed from English or Afrikaans as possible – in case the SA tax people should start an investigation.

Friewi and I motored back along the Rhine in a very relaxed frame of mind. But was it hot. In our countryside stopovers I tried each night to have a bath. I found that the German country folk apparently were not bath-minded. Invariably there was either no bathroom, or else the bathroom key could not be found or, if it was found, the bath on one occasion was full of coal. I usually managed to scrounge a bath somehow – but at an extra cost of five DM. Friewi, with Germanic indifference, could not be bothered to bath. I think he was secretly surprised at my insistence on keeping clean. When we arrived back in Düsseldorf after a week's absence Friewi said casually, 'I think I take a bath.' My only remark was, 'About time too.'

I reported fully on the Liechtenstein adventure at the next meeting, and they were satisfied that I had solved the tax difficulty. Luftverkeers Anstalt became an integral part of Trek for the next twenty years. Twice a year I sojourned in Vaduz to fix up our annual accounts. Everyone was happy.

Bombshell

By June 1954 Trek had been in operation for six months. All departments were working satisfactorily and efficiently. Tax was no longer a problem. Our meetings were pleasant, harmonious and productive. For the first time we all felt that from now on we could relax a bit, and just attend to our day-to-day needs. The profits were starting to mount, the bank balance was no problem. How wrong we were.

At a board meeting towards the end of June, Fanie, from the chair, opened the proceedings with an important announcement. 'Gentlemen, I have good news. I have managed to sell the DC-3 in England for £25,000. It only cost us £15,000 to build up, so we make a profit of £10,000 – not bad after six months.' We were flabbergasted. Then the truth came out.

Pongola Sugar Estates

Fanie Botha, after investing his £15,000 in Trek and also guaranteeing for us a sizeable overdraft for working capital, had apparently, like Alexander the Great of old, looked round for fresh worlds to conquer. He decided on Pongola, which was a vast sugar-growing area. From a mate of his in the Broedersbond (where Fanie had now risen to be deputy leader in the Transvaal) he gleaned that the government had a plan afoot to take over large tracts of sugar country for a special purpose, and that the farmers would be paid out handsomely for their ground – therefore sugar farming soil was at a premium and selling at a high price. His informant was Senator Conroy, Minister of Lands. Fanie resolved to become a sugar farmer in Pongola overnight – as long as the cane was in the ground the government would have to pay market price for the ground. Fanie invested heavily in farming property, taking out an overdraft from his bank – within six months the ground would be sold and the liability to the bank liquidated. No problem.

He tackled the task of converting open veld into sugar country with the same verve and determination that he had applied to 'Huggins' Folly' in Rhodesia. A large labour force, working round the clock, at night under floodlights, intent only in giving the soil the appearance of a sugar farm. As long as he could hoodwink the government valuators he would reap a rich harvest in far less time than the cane would take to mature. Then came disaster – the cabinet turned down the senator's pipe dream. Overnight the value of Pongola farms slumped. Fanie must have had nightmares about rocks and hard places. The bank swooped, calling up the overdraft. Fanie's cash flow had dried up – no cash, no flow. His only lifeboat was the Trek loan of £15,000. It had to be repaid, and by yesterday. In 1954 £15,000 was a fortune, not the 'petty cash' that it is today. Fanie's promise to Trek went by the way – having scruples had never been his strong point.

Exit Fanie Botha

When Fanie made his dramatic demand to the board, none of us had an inkling of the Pongola disaster. Not that it would have helped; Fanie was in headlong flight – unstoppable. When asked by what authority he had contracted to sell the DC-3, he replied, 'I am the managing director, and I can run the company as I see fit.' I then delivered a knockout blow. I explained to the meeting that the Companies Act had been amended in 1952 to make it illegal for any officer of a company, including the managing director, to sell any major asset without the consent of at least 75% of the shareholders. Fanie saw red. He physically stormed at me, but luckily I was still agile enough to elude him, until the others could contain him. We put the matter to the vote and Fanie's proposition was unanimously defeated. We explained to him that the purpose of Trek was to run an airline, not to dabble in aircraft – in any case we had hundreds of pax lined up who had paid their deposits. In fact, the plane was even now standing ready at Jan Smuts to take off tomorrow with a full complement. Fanie raved that unless we agreed to the immediate sale when the plane landed in England, tomorrow's flight would not take off. We refused, and he ran out shouting that he was taking legal action to call up his loan, which was only a verbal undertaking with him – we had trusted him.

From then on things moved rapidly. Within a half-hour our fuel suppliers, Shell, phoned urgently to say that our bank was going to dishonour our cheque to them for the fuel carnet. Fanie had withdrawn his guarantee for the bank overdraft. We were unanimous that Fanie would not wreck Trek. Tomorrow's flight must take off on time.

Even though by now it was after 5 p.m. I phoned Shell back and promised a new cheque on another bank which would be met tomorrow. It was lucky that we had opened a separate account with another bank for the deposits in the name of Luftverkeers

Anstalt. We had never thought it important to tell Fanie of this account – he was never interested in the day-to-day affairs of Trek. Shell was adamant; they had withdrawn our carnet. Later we learned that Fanie had considerable influence with Shell, as he was a shareholder. I immediately phoned Mobil Oil – would they be interested in becoming our fuel supplier and could they arrange a carnet first thing on the morrow? Of course – they were only too happy to land such a contract. But it would take a few hours to issue it.

I then suggested that Vyv Graham, tomorrow's flight captain, be instructed to take off without a carnet – we would send it posthaste up the route when it was ready. In the meanwhile he was to use the usual float of £4,000, which every captain carried on a flight to pay cash for hotel accommodation and incidental expenses, to buy fuel. This would be an unheard-of procedure in normal circumstances, but this was an emergency. It was essential that the flight be in the air no later than 6 a.m. so that Fanie could not get a court injunction to stop the flight, as he had threatened. We later heard that Fanie had indeed visited a judge at his residence to try to get an immediate court order to stop the flight taking off, as it would endanger the security for his loan to Trek. The judge would not act immediately, as he found no reason for urgency. He would examine it in the morning. Vyv took off promptly at 6 a.m., the fuel carnet reached him two days later and Fanie was utterly defeated.

The matter could not of course rest there, as a court order might prevent us from flying. Sadly we agreed to compromise with Fanie. We would allow the plane to be sold in thirty days' time, so as to allow us in the interim to acquire a replacement. Fanie would resign, and surrender his shares. He was out. Exit Fanie Botha.

When Rod Rooken-Smith, now in East London, heard the news of both Syd Excel and Fanie Botha, he felt that there was no longer any point in him remaining as a shareholder, and he put his shares up for sale. We accepted, and so now I was the sole survivor of the original four musketeers – sad, but in the long run it all turned out for the best. Man proposes...

The board had for a while been considering it wise to bring in a deputy for Tom Meredith in operations – in the flying game you never know what can happen. Accidents do happen!

Tom proposed a pilot who had a good war record in the SA Air Force, a stable character by the name of Cecil Snelgar. We offered him Rod's shares, and he accepted with alacrity. He came onto the board. A new era had begun.

Aircraft Re-equipment

Jock Hamilton's value to Trek was never better illustrated than when it came to acquiring a substitute for our beloved DC-3, which had served us so well and reliably. Finance we now had, in the form of the profit from Fanie's sale, as well as the profits which had accrued over the successful six months' flying. Even after repaying Fanie we had enough to put down against a purchase. Jock scoured the overseas aircraft markets, and within a surprisingly short time came to light with a bargain. He bought three Vikings in a package deal. Despite having fabric wings, they proved no less reliable than the old DC-3. We now had three for the price of one. It afforded Trek much more versatility – Fred no longer had to rush aircraft maintenance schedules through with expensive overtime, and could do his jobs at a more leisurely pace. Furthermore we now had spare planes for emergencies, and could quote for ad hoc charter flights to anywhere in the world. We were no longer restricted to one European trip each week. Helm's department had more diversified canvassing to do, and Tom had to employ extra crews. Upward and onward for Trek!

Over the years the Vikings served Trek well until the time arrived when SA Airways went jet, and graciously allowed Trek to graduate to four-engined crafts – something which was denied us by the NTC for many years. We only had one minor setback with the Vikings, when a bird flew into the fabric wing and we had to make an emergency landing at Pietersburg – but there was no great hassle, no one hurt and no long delay in sending a relief aircraft. In retrospect Fanie Botha really did Trek a favour by disposing of the Dakota. And we no longer had the threat of a possible loan repayment hanging over our heads.

Chairman

It was one of life's coincidences that just at the time that Fanie departed we were being pestered by the mayor of Johannesburg to allow him to come into Trek. He had been given a complimentary flight for propaganda purposes, and was so impressed that he wanted to be part of us. In retrospect we realised that what he was really after was more complimentary flights. Charles Patmore was a smooth talker, the leader of the United Party in the Transvaal and a man of infinite persuasion. We all fell for him.

He could not at that time pay for his shares, as he had an important deal pending – it would take a little time. We were all too naive, and took him in as chairman in place of Fanie Botha. His overseas jaunts became frequent and had little to do with Trek's business. Moreover, reports began to reach us that he was not without amorous inclinations when out of the country – this despite a rather agreeable wife as well as a family. In fact in Johannesburg he had built up a name as being the ideal family man – he was even chairman of a marriage counselling bureau. The only discernible advantage that we at Trek ever derived from Charles Patmore was the occasional ride in Johannesburg's mayoral Rolls Royce. We were soon disillusioned with him.

When after a few months of ineffective talking and no money from him, we decided that Mr Charles Patmore was, at best, a damp squib, and we sent him on his way.

We had now lost faith in Lord Mayors, and agreed that the time had come to go non-mayor. We felt that it would be unfair to saddle the head of any department, who was occupied full-time, with the responsibilities of chairmanship. Of all the directors, I was the only one who was only part-time – I was still conducting my auditing practice. The board therefore voted to make Paddy Rorke the next chairman – after all, I was the only founder member left in Trek. This position I had for the next quarter of a century, and Trek Airways went from strength to strength.

John Foggitt and TFC

Over the years Trek had on many occasions to attend hearings of the NTC – either to apply for more flights or larger aircraft (usually fruitlessly) or else to object to the granting of any new competitive licence. Cecil Margo and myself became buddies in opposition to each other – only on the same side when opposing any newcomer. He was always the perfect gentleman and I could not but admire and respect him. No wonder that he later made such an excellent judge.

It was in Trek's early years that I had to oppose an applicant for a charter licence. It was an unusual case because the applicant was unknown in aviation circles. The aviation world is an intimate one and most operators are recognised by the other operators. That day we were objecting to a man that none of us had ever come across before – Mr John Foggitt.

He did not employ counsel, and he expertly presented his own case. Margo and myself both opposed him and his application was summarily turned down by the NTC. But the man's whole manner and method of address impressed me. Consequently as we emerged from the hearing I invited him to coffee in a nearby cafe. I learned the reason for his application. His two sons and a party of local boy scouts wanted to attend a jamboree to be held in England, and if he were to own a charter plane he could take the whole troop of scouts to the UK. Furthermore, he was contemplating starting a business bringing new young immigrants to South Africa. He wanted to build up our country – a noble ideal. I offered his two sons each a complimentary fare to attend their jamboree, which he accepted with gratitude. It was the character of John Foggitt that prompted my offer – but I did not realise at the time that this gesture was to reap hundredfold benefits both for Trek and for me personally.

It was not long after that John Foggitt resigned his government position in the auditor-general's office and went into business on his own account.

When issuing to him his two complimentary tickets I learned that he resided in Irene, and travelled by train each day to Johannesburg to set up his new office. In those days, so soon after the end of the war, petrol was still not plentiful and so I also travelled to Johannesburg each Friday for our board meetings. We formed the habit of sitting together on the railway and chatting. I got to know and respect him even more than at first.

He was busy setting up an enterprise called South African Immigration Organisation (Samorgan). Its purpose would be to canvass overseas for young immigrants to settle in South Africa, mainly from the UK and the continent, particularly Germany, where thousands of young men had seen the end of hostilities with no immediate prospect of making a living. His main recruiting office would be in London, and he was looking for a South African to run this office in the UK.

I had a brother who worked for Iscor in Pretoria, and who had recently returned from a visit to England. He was hugely impressed and was dying to work in London. Bryan was a few years my junior, and was a keen sportsman, excelling at school at cricket, and who later became a good golfer. He had an attractive personality and I thought that he would be an excellent person for the job. Besides, it would be a marvellous opportunity to return to England.

I recommended him for John Foggitt's new London office. Bryan landed up in his beloved London, where he happily spent the rest of his life.

Samorgan took off and whenever Trek had spare accommodation, the young immigrants were flown to their new home by Trek Airways. Many loads of young Germans under the age of twenty-five were brought in for the mines in the Union. My association with John Foggitt was paying off. Not many months later on one of our train journeys, John told me laughingly that he was about to start a 'joke club'. His projected name was 'Travellers' Facilities Club'. 'Bit of a mouthful,' I remarked, 'why not simply TFC?' And TFC it was. In the years to come, TFC grew into South Africa's largest, most efficient and most popular way of holidaying overseas. John Foggitt turned out to be one of the most efficient, most imaginative and most industrious travel organisers in South African history. A more likeable and pleasant person you could never meet. I have never ceased to admire his ability. Thousands of South African trippers still today owe many of their overseas holidays to John Foggitt and TFC. Trek on many occasions carried out special charter flights for him to far-off destinations. I personally owe to John many of my overseas holidays either by air or by cruise – visits that I normally might never have made to the Seychelles, Mauritius, the Greek islands and even to Japan. TFC always offered me complimentary journeys, always with the pick of accommodation – once even the Royal Suite. Dear John – what a man!

Jock Hamilton and the Safari Club

Jock Hamilton established his London office on the first floor of a building just half a block off Trafalgar Square, above the Silver Cross, a typical little English pub where we used to enjoy bar lunches. In 1957 Jock said that the time had come for Trek to publicise its image with downstairs premises. We at home were dubious, but Jock was never without his typical Scottish doggedness. He came to us with what we thought was an ambitious idea, of some property which had fallen vacant in the well-known Northumberland Grand Building right in the heart of Trafalgar Square, opposite South Africa House. There was on offer a downstairs office on Northumberland Avenue, a cellar and three large rooms on the first floor. Much too large, our board thought, because all this accommodation had to be taken up and the lease had to be for twenty years. Madness, said we! Jock left on the very next flight. He vehemently urged that this was an opportunity of a lifetime, not to be missed.

He was adamant that if his plan flopped, there would be no difficulty in finding someone to sublet from us. He undertook to guarantee and organise this, should the occasion arise. He then disclosed his master plan. He wanted to establish a club on the first floor, with a bar in the basement. Clubs in London could only make money, and Trek would have a street window right in the heart of London's busiest centre, Trafalgar Square. He talked a hole in our respective heads and we signed the lease with crossed fingers and doubt in our hearts. Jock had won.

Jock worked feverishly for many weeks and the club was opened, the offices on the ground floor ready.

Those of us who had come to know Jock were amazed at his activity. Normally it was difficult to get Jock to the office before 10.30 – as befits a true English executive. It was his Scottish upbringing that gave him the drive when it was really needed. No wonder he earned two high war decorations. A remarkable character! The club we named the Safari Club (very South African). My brother Bryan, working for Samorgan and John Foggitt, said his job was coming to an end as Foggitt was now winding Samorgan down in favour of TFC. Jock offered Bryan managership of the Safari Club, which he accepted. In addition Jock's energetic and lovely wife, a Scottish lass named Flo, came in to do the catering.

It was largely Bryan's organisation that brought in performers for the cabarets, and Bryan really ran the day-to-day activities of the club. Bryan had been well known in sporting circles in South Africa, and consequently attracted many South African visitors to the club. So much so, that he had to cope with constant offers of drinks from Springbok supporters in London. He found a solution. The barman was instructed never to serve a gin and ginger beer. It had to be water and ginger beer, as this was Bryan's drink. For months this scheme worked well, but one day a misguided South African actually ordered gin and ginger beer. Bryan had to do a lot of apologising.

Over the years the Safari Club attracted a good membership and earned the reputation of being an 'in' London club. Situated as it was opposite South Africa House and next door to the War Office and New Scotland Yard, it drew many elite business figures. The basement bar was invariably crowded at lunchtime and in the early evenings after office hours. Turnover was good, and two slot machines brought in a regular £400 to £500 per month – this at sixpence a throw – those were the days! There it was that I learned how slots could be manipulated. Should the machines not be making money, we simply asked the lessors to lessen the payouts. Should they not be attracting custom by poor payouts we asked for them to be adjusted upwards. Can the punter ever win? The club certainly did!

Bryan's main duty was to develop the entertainment area on the first floor. He furnished the large rooms attractively, and this showed good hire income from weddings, dances and other types of amusement. When the space was not in demand Bryan staged regular nightly cabarets – music, entertainers and dancing girls of high quality. Nothing shoddy or vulgar. Many rising London comedians made their debut in the Safari Club. There was a well-known tour organiser, Prang Russell, who used to end each tour by depositing his sightseers at the Safari Club – quite a fair source of revenue for the club.

Prang had a partner who had a teenage son, fifteen years of age, who was thinking of forming a small band and had ambitions as he professed to sing. Prang urged us to allow Paul Gadd to perform. The music from the youngster was, to my ears, ghastly – but then I am no connoisseur of contemporary so-called music. One night, I was having a drink and a conversation with Prang and a BBC producer, when the subject turned to modern music. The producer boasted that he could take a boy off the street and turn him into a star within six months. Prang then suggested he should try it with Paul – the producer agreed. About six months later, a single record was made by Paul Raven, and he appeared on, I think, a 1965 special on BBC. I must have again been very wrong in my musical judgement, because not many years later this selfsame singer hit the top of the pops in the UK under the pseudonym of 'Gary Glitter'. Many years later, I saw and heard Gary Glitter on TV, and recognised him as Paul Gadd. He made millions, and became one of the top British stars for some years. I never again saw him, but the press recently reported that he had fallen on evil times. It certainly brought back memories. I felt sorry about that, but I unfortunately never became a lover of extremely modern music.

Our ideally situated London premises earned much prestige for Trek. To the English, prestige is a sought-after virtue – especially if you cannot rise to a Rolls. Jock's dream was completely vindicated.

The club flourished until 1961 when South Africa withdrew from the Commonwealth. Rabble-rousers burnt down our club, leaving the rest of Northumberland Grand untouched. The street-front office we quickly repaired and thus we lost little trade. The below-level bar was saved, but to restore the first floor entertainment area took almost two years. To get new plans passed by the London County Council is more painful than teeth extraction and even more frustrating. All doors had to be fireproof – shades of the London war blitz. Bryan was unemployed but found new employment still in London, where he remained right up to the time that he retired. We decided not to open the entertainment area, which was sublet, but retained the underground bar, which kept on attracting members and custom.

For me personally the club was a home from home during my frequent visits. There was always a warm welcome awaiting me, and I spent many happy hours meeting local business executives and understanding that their approach to their calling was so different to ours in South Africa – not so intent, more relaxed and leisurely, and more trustworthy than many of their counterparts in our country. I recall one occasion when I had to call on Lombard Bank, to arrange an overdraft for six million pounds for an aircraft which we were buying from America. Our local Barclays Bank (today First National Bank) had kept me waiting for weeks on end trying to process the advance. I grew tired and decided to try Lombard Bank who had advertised in our local press. I found the general manager easily approachable (not like in SA). Mr Osbourne was charm itself and when I explained in detail my mission he replied, 'Yes, that will be all right.' He promptly went on to a long dissertation about the round-the-world trip from which he had only yesterday returned. He waxed vehement when he told me that the British tax authorities had not allowed him to claim as a business expense a two-day stopover, which he had made in Hawaii to rest up after a hectic business schedule. When he had finished his tirade, he offered me a drink as it was now 12.30. No respectable UK executive worked after the lunch hour started. 'But,' I said to Mr Osbourne, 'should we not first sign all the necessary documents?' His immediate reply was, 'Just send us the invoice and I shall see that it is paid.' Could that ever happen in South Africa?

What I particularly enjoyed about the dear old Safari Club was that I could spend many happy hours of my spare time in London watching all types of sport. This is why I always arranged to make one trip overseas during July, the height of the London summer season with Wimbledon, British Open Golf, Henley Regatta, and Lord's Test Match, because these were the days when Cabinet Minister Hertzog was avidly trying to protect the gullible South African public from the 'horror' of television.

Yes, Jock's visionary foresight enabled the British public and also overseas visitors to London to become aware of Trek's fabulous flights, so different from ordinary, humdrum air travel.

Four Engines

As the years rolled by the three Vikings continued to serve us well and faithfully. We did in fact manage in due course to persuade the NTC to allow us additional weekly flights and were allowed to fly twice per week to Europe. But four-engined aircraft – neither the NTC nor SA Airways would hear of, until the jet era arrived. Once SA Airways had converted to jets it was no longer fair for Trek not to be able also to modernise. At last we acquired a four-engined Douglas DC-4. The Vikings were disposed of, and as a back-up aircraft we imported a long-range Super Constellation from the States. On its delivery flight it flew empty direct from Seattle to Hamburg; it was in the air continuously for twenty-two hours.

This plane made a bit of history for Trek. It was the time when SA Airways were opening up their service to Australia with their newly-acquired Boeing 707s.

Unfortunately their aircraft had not yet arrived on the date when the new service was scheduled to commence. They already had passengers booked. In desperation they chartered our Connie until their plane should arrive. So Trek carried out the inaugural first SAA flights to Australia – in all, eleven such trips! Quite a prestige for us, and it tended to sweeten our relationship with the national airline – a relationship which over the years kept on improving.

Our Trek board felt that the time must be approaching when we too should be allowed to follow the world trend to jets. We took a momentous and brave decision. We placed an order with Boeing in Seattle for a new 707. The delivery was only two years ahead, during which time the plane was being assembled. The price was six million pounds. We paid a deposit of one million, and committed ourselves to a large quarterly instalment during the build-up period.

As the delivery was at hand and we had not yet managed to get the NTC to allow us to operate jets, a miracle saved us. A 707 of SA Airways crashed at Windhoek – SAA's first tragedy. A replacement, as we all knew, took two years to build up in America. Their fleet was short, and they could in no way meet their commitments. In desperation they again approached Trek – 'Please sell us your new 707.' We were in the driving seat. We agreed, but only if they agreed to sell us one of their old 707s, whose range was too short for their purposes – and further, that they supported our application to the NTC to use a jet. They were in our hands and Trek acquired its first jet. A whole new world had now opened up to us.

Apartheid Sanctions

After the teething troubles with Sydney, Fanie Botha and Charles Patmore, Trek settled down to six years of steady growth, safe flying and image-building, and firmly established its place as second only to SA Airways in serving the African route. Danie Joubert, chairman of the all-governing NTC, had once suggested that there should always be a second SA carrier on the route, so as to provide a measure of competition. That is why Trek was a favoured licensee, and why other applicants had little chance of getting an oar in the water. Also, it was still too soon for the national airlines of the European countries to be able to organise overseas services – but they were all waiting in the wings: BOAC, Lufthansa, Air France, KLM and the rest.

Trek cruised along comparatively unhindered until 1959. We had acquired additional flights, and larger aircraft, and we were feeling quietly relaxed, with our regular Friday board meetings running smoothly. The garden was lovely. Suddenly a cloud appeared on the horizon. Sanctions against the SA apartheid regime were beginning to bite. More and more countries were joining the race to isolate South Africa. With a bump, we at Trek realised that any day in the near future African states might withdraw our overflying rights. Already SAA was no longer landing anywhere on the continent – they were going direct to Ile de Sol. This option was, however, denied to us as the extra fuel cost of such a roundabout route would make our operation uneconomical. The additional fuel bill worked out at 25% higher than at present – and already the cost of fuel was on a constant rise. We had to discard our South African image – but how? The obvious solution was similar to the one that we had found in establishing Luftverkeers Anstalt.

We could only solve the problem by registering a completely separate company overseas, while retaining Trek's licence privileges in South Africa, but discarding the name of Trek.

In my ignorance, I approached the Liechtenstein Minister of Transport and enquired about an airbase in Vaduz. 'Mr Rorke,' he replied to my query, 'do you realise that if we were to build an international airport in our country the beginning of the runway would have to be in Switzerland and the end of the runway would land up in Germany? Further, the towering Alpine mountains would make it the most dangerous landing strip in the world – even worse than Hong Kong.' I left cap in hand.

Jock busied himself researching the European possibilities, but most countries were about to establish their own national airline – they wanted no competition. Only Luxembourg might be a solution. Jock, sometimes assisted by Tom, started to curry favour with the local Luxair. We were relieved to find out that Luxair had no African aspirations – they were happy to operate round Europe. Yes, they were planning a larger international airport as Luxembourg was fast taking on international status. Jock worked tirelessly on them.

To establish landing rights between two countries requires a reciprocal agreement at government level. Each country must acquire landing rights into the other country on an equal basis. Should we succeed in persuading the Luxembourg Minister of Transport to come to South Africa to negotiate such a reciprocal agreement, it would only be sanctioned by our NTC if the rights of flights into South Africa from Luxembourg were ceded to Trek's nominee – if Luxembourg insisted on retaining these landings in SA for themselves, the SA NTC would not allow it – it would be in competition to SAA. A tricky problem.

Jock negotiated with Luxembourg for two years, but eventually won them over. The Minister would journey to South Africa, would sign a reciprocal agreement with SA and, most important of all, would cede their flights to Trek's nominee. It was a mammoth achievement by Jock. We decided that the new company to take over from Trek would be called Luxavia – we even managed to persuade Luxair not to object to a name similar to theirs.

Trek was mothballed, and Luxavia took over. And only just in time, because African overfly rights were almost immediately withdrawn from SA carriers. In fact our very flight under the banner of Luxavia was stopped in Cairo, as our crews were recognised as being South Africans. We could not convince them that Luxavia was not a South African company – in fact we had to call on the Luxembourg government to intervene and demand that they release our plane.

For the rest of our existence we were known as Luxavia, and established very cordial relations with the Luxembourg authorities. Another hazard had been overcome – thanks mostly to Jock Hamilton. Viva Luxavia! The final agreement gave South Africa fifty-two flights per annum into South Africa, which Luxair ceded to Luxavia. Consequently we were allowed 104 flights per annum – two each week. We scheduled them for take-off each Tuesday and each Friday. It was a very satisfactory arrangement.

Joggie Vermooten – Rentmeester Beleggings Bpk

Our new Luxavia directorate (the same as the old Trek) was once again prone to complacency. What more could ever go wrong? Surely we had had our fill of surprises and shocks. It was a comforting notion, but a very wrong one.

The next hiccup came when some time later I arrived back from one of my usual overseas tours of the various offices on the continent and, of course, London. I had been away for almost a month. As I alighted from the steps at Jan Smuts I was surprised to see not only Fred to welcome me as always, but with him the General and Cecil Snelgar as well. I smelt a rat. What could it be now? With worried faces they hustled me into a reception lounge, and started gabbling that Tom had buggered up Trek.

The story unfolded. In my absence there had been a hearing of the NTC, and Luxavia had to oppose an application for a new charter licence. In the past I was the only one ever to appear on these occasions for Trek, now Luxavia. Tom, with a swagger that we had always associated with Captain Meredith, had said that he was quite capable of doing what I usually did at hearings. The board let him appear, despite him having no knowledge of Afrikaans. But this was not the problem as the hearing was conducted in English. 'So what happened, what is there to worry about?' asked I.

During Tom's address he had apparently made some statement that the chairman did not agree with. Tom lost his cool and called Danie Joubert a liar. Fur flew. Eventually the application was turned down, but Danie Joubert closed the hearing with the remark that he hoped that Tom would never again appear before him.

To the casual observer, this incident may not appear to be very significant. But the surrounding political circumstances at the time should be realised. The South African government was now in full swing with its apartheid policy – the world was against them. Our company was now registered outside the Union, and was composed mainly of foreigners – English and German. I was the only *egte-Afrikaans* member – the only one who could speak Afrikaans. The Minister of Transport was Ben Schoeman, who had the power to grant or revoke any charter licence without a right to appeal to the courts. Therefore it would be easy for him, if he so wished, to put Luxavia out of business and grant a new charter licence to a Broedersbond-related concern. We no longer had the influence of Fanie Botha. The Minister would not hesitate to do Danie Joubert's bidding. Therefore we were in the hands of Danie, and if he should turn vindictive we could be folded up overnight. They told me that I must do something, pronto. They had no suggestions, but I must come up with an idea.

After much soul-searching, I decided on a course of action. We must restore to Trek a Broedersbond element, or at least a pro-government supporter.

I had for many years lectured in Accounting at Pretoria University. I regularly had two classes each week, which involved some 200 students per annum. The medium was Afrikaans with the result that over many years I had built up a good relationship with students who later graduated to important posts in the Civil Service. For example, the governor of the Reserve Bank had at one time been in my class. I knew that somewhere amongst my ex-students there must be a man who had graduated to government influence, and who would be a useful member for our company.

I hit on the ideal solution. It was a man who had obtained his B.Com through my hands, and had become one of Pretoria's leading chartered accountants. He had been lucky to be articled to a firm of two aged CAs who had both passed away with no family. Joggie inherited their practice before he was qualified as a CA (SA). He had asked my assistance to help him to sign balance sheets until such time as he became qualified to do so. With the consent of the Transvaal Society of Accountants I had assisted him and he was grateful. Furthermore, Joggie had a most agreeable, pleasant personality, and was a man of principle and thoroughly reliable. That he had influence with the government I had no doubt – he was the state-appointed director of Iscor, South Africa's largest steelworks. I knew that he addressed cabinet ministers by their Christian names. Whether or not he was a Broederbonder I was not sure, but it was unlikely that he was not. I liked the man. In addition he had established an investment on the Johannesburg Stock Exchange called Rentmeester Beleggings Bpk. I recommended him to the board, none of whom knew him.

So I approached Joggie Vermooten and offered his company an investment in Luxavia (Pty) Ltd. We had long discussions and eventually Joggie agreed to take a 25% interest and to come onto the board. I think that my co-directors were expecting a dour, lacklustre Afrikaner when I introduced them to Joggie. They were more than pleasantly surprised – Joggie greeted them with a winning smile, and soon displayed a fine sense of humour, as well as an astute business brain.

Over the years we grew not only to respect Joggie Vermooten but very much to like him, and looked forward to our weekly meetings with him on the board. More importantly, we now knew that we were safe from any onslaught from Ben Schoeman. Once again we could afford to be complacent, and this time the feeling persisted for many years ahead. At last we had cleared the final hurdle and the winning tape was not far ahead. Hooray!

Berlin, 1937: Members of the War Academy at a State Dinner given by Hitler in the Reichs Chancellery. Mellenthin is third from Hitler's left

Copy of Von Mellenthin

Princesses Elizabeth and Margaret, 1947

Mimi Coertse, 1950

Captain Meredith, 1970

Train used by royal family in South Africa, 1947

Royal family, Salisbury Airport, 1947

Queen Mother, Administrator Pienaar and Princess Elizabeth, 1947

Von Mellenthin and Friewi, ninetieth birthday

Evelyn and Joggie Vermooten

Walter Battiss

Jock and Paddy Ashley, Clinton Manor

TFC tour, Paddy and Yvonne boarding Danae

Yvonne and Paddy in cabin of Danae

Ben Schoeman, has highway named after him between Pretoria and Johannesburg

Justice Margo, who played a very important part in the Transport Commission

*Model of 'Trek' over Johannesburg.
Paddy owned the model that was used*

One of Trek Airways Fleet Viking Aircraft "LOUIS TRICHARDT" *ZS-DKI*

Bryan Rorke

J G Foggitt

Cecil Snelgar

Fred Gratz

Paddy Rorke seated in the Viking, front right

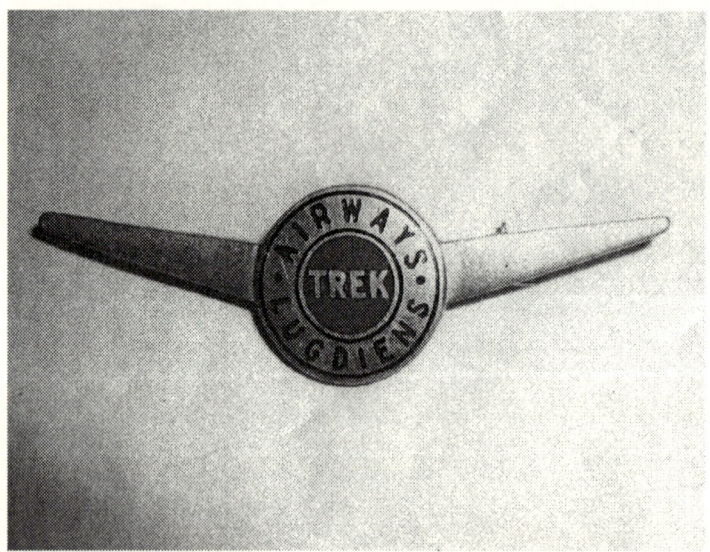
Trek Airways badge, Joe Calafato, inscribed on rear

Minister Ben Schoeman & Danie Joubert

I have already mentioned the names of Ben Schoeman and Danie Joubert. Perhaps I should explain my relationships with these two gentlemen, both enthusiastic supporters of the apartheid government and ardent Broederbonders, I have no doubt. No outsider ever really knew who was a Broederbonder and who was not, except the members themselves. Membership was a closed book, a secret association, but in those days all-powerful – they controlled the destiny of South Africa.

I first encountered, but did not actually meet, Danie Joubert in my university days in 1931 in Grahamstown, Rhodes University. We were hosting the inter-varsity annual athletics meeting. In the Stellenbosch team was the South African one hundred yards record holder, a man of nineteen named Danie Joubert. The prize event of the gathering would be the one hundred yards sprint. We watched in amazement as the tall, heavily built Danie Joubert sped past the tape to break the world record, in 9.4 seconds – a record which stood for many years. I was an insignificant *'ink'* ('nothing', from the Greek *inkus*), but luckily took a snapshot of Danie breasting the tape – the only picture of this momentous occasion. When Tom affronted Danie Joubert, now chairman of the NTC, I dug up my old photo album and enlarged the snapshot of the race, then I set it in an attractive frame. I sent it to Danie at Christmas time with a short note, as by now he and I were well acquainted from many hearings of the NTC. He was thrilled and thanked me profusely, as he had no record of his achievement. For me it was a peace-offering – how he regarded it, I never found out, but it cemented our relationship, and I always felt that he gave me a slightly more considerate hearing than others. Normally he was straight from the shoulder, forthright and sometimes verging on rudeness in his conduct of the meetings. He certainly disconcerted naive applicants appearing before him for the first time. It was because Tom was brash enough not to appear to be humbled by the overpowering Danie, that there was a brush. In my dealings with the NTC I was always more tactful, and we always got on well together.

As far as Minister Ben Schoeman was concerned I made it my duty to try and become well acquainted with him from the early days of Trek – I was under no illusions about his influence with the NTC. Luckily his younger wife, Herculene, was an avid bridge player – my wife met her over the card table. We started asking her home for a hand of cards, and developed a social connection. I suggested that she and my wife make an overseas trip on Trek – complimentary, of course. My wife reported that it was a great success. Herculene was a lively soul, even dancing on the table one night in a German nightclub. We were accepted into the Schoeman circle, and attended many functions in their residence in Bryntirion in Pretoria. On one occasion most of the cabinet was having cocktails in their lounge when the prime minister called them to the nearby Union buildings. I was the only non-cabinet man present. I tried not to listen to their heated discussions about their visit, as I did not think it to be in my province to hear apparently private discussions.

On occasions we had Oom Ben to dinner. Promptly at quarter to eight he would produce his waistcoat watch and say, 'Time to eat.' He was nothing if not forthright – I liked him. He was always early to bed and left just after the port. Funnily enough, despite being a staunch Afrikaner, he would not drink South African port – 'We don't know how to make port in this country,' was always his remark.

Only once did I have an uncomfortable experience with Oom Ben. Before each parliamentary session in Cape Town I used to have lunch with a golfing pal of mine – Dr Frans Cronje, the United member in parliament for Jeppe in Johannesburg. Frans was the shadow opposition's transport minister, and he wanted me to keep him up to date with aviation developments in the country. One such day I told him about a rumour that Ben Schoeman's wife had an interest in an opposition airline, which was being operated out of Lourenco Marques (Maputo) by a Greek company. I promised to post a full report of anything that I could glean in this connection to Frans in Cape Town – which I duly did.

Nothing of this was ever mentioned during the session, and I asked Frans on his return whether he had received my letter. He had, but did not have the opportunity to raise it as the session had closed early. Not long after, a summons came to Trek that the minister wanted to see Mr Rorke in his office in the Union buildings – alone.

This was before the advent of Joggie Vermooten, and all the board members insisted on accompanying me. They were plainly scared – could this affect our licence? The minister wanted only me, and would not admit the others. I was surprised, and not a little uneasy, to hear him address me formally as Mr Rorke, instead of the usual Paddy. There was a male secretary present, taking notes. Ben produced a large file, and read from a letter in it – it was my letter to Frans, word for word. As he read, he passed comments: 'This is wrong,' and so on. What was also disconcerting was that he spoke to me in English whereas we usually spoke Afrikaans to each other. When he had finished reading he said, 'I suppose that you realise that I have a libel action against you for what you have written.'

'No, Mr Minister,' I said. 'That letter is a confidential communication address to a member of parliament and not for publication.' He could not refute it, and realised that he was wrong. I apologised for anything which was incorrect, and we called a truce. The matter was never again referred to, and we both forgot it. It did not affect our future relationship. To this date I cannot fathom how the letter got into the minister's hands. Frans certainly did not give it to him. It just confirms for me that in those apartheid years there must have been a systematic scheme of state eavesdropping.

It is interesting to note that this same Dr Frans Cronje became chairman of SA Breweries, one of SA's largest and most influential holding companies. Before the days of Joggie Vermooten I had approached Frans from SAB and Nedbank to come into Trek, but then I realised that they did not have the necessary political clout – both Frans and his companies were plainly United Party orientated. Marvellous how politics governs our lives – business as well as private.

How could anyone in those days ever have imagined that

many, many years later when driving along South Africa's busiest highway, the M1 from Pretoria to Johannesburg, one would find it divided into two sections dedicated to those two stalwarts of the apartheid era, Danie Joubert and Ben Schoeman – two men with whom from time to time I had been involved over a lifetime stretching back to 1931 in Grahamstown over sixty years ago? Thus is the absolute unpredictability of nostalgic existence!

Diversions

During Trek's chequered history there were two forays into other fields that occurred – both were bitter disappointments.

The first was in our early days before the Joggie Vermooten era when John Foggitt and I used to get together for chats on scattered occasions. Over the years after the launching of TFC, I had formed a firm opinion that John was an exceptional personality, a shrewd and gifted businessman and a thoroughly likeable and trustworthy person. There had been many charters carried out by Trek on behalf of TFC, with profit to both, and never a hitch. It was my secret dream that one day we might be able to draw his ability into the Trek set-up. He sensed my thinking. So one day we discussed the possibility of some sort of closer cooperation between our two companies. TFC, even in those early days, was beginning to flourish – the public had taken to it, and when John staged a reception for all persons who had been on TFC tours once a year, it was handsomely attended by patrons arriving from all over the Union to meet with John Foggitt face to face. A wonderfully inspired gimmick which only John could have thought out. The profits of TFC were rocketing. Trek's earnings were rising, but I was sure that they did not equate to that of TFC. John and I never discussed profits – we were more interested in building an empire.

One day we eventually got together on the matter of an interchange of shareholdings. With great difficulty and much reluctance on their part I managed to persuade my co-directors to meet for a round table with John Foggitt. They had all dealt with him on many occasions, particularly to arrange charters, so they knew him. But I always felt that they were diffident towards him because of a slight inferiority complex – he was quick-thinking, forthright and direct, but not in any way aggressive or overbearing in manner of action. They felt, I think, overawed. We met. After a long and thorough discussion it was agreed that Trek would offer him a seventh interest in return for a half share in TFC – better than I had ever imagined.

Trek would make more profit on paper out of the deal, and John was too shrewd not to realise it – but it meant much to TFC to have aircraft on tap at a moment's notice. It suited both sides. I rode back to Pretoria singing. I looked forward to having such a good business brain at our Friday meetings. But at ten o'clock at home that evening the phone rang.

The others wanted to pull out of the deal. They told me that I must explain to Foggitt. They would say no more except, 'He is too clever for us.' Ridiculous – can you ever imagine not wanting to be associated with someone because he is too clever? Only if he is untrustworthy as well, which John most definitely was not. I was more than shamefaced when I explained to John that the deal was off – I told him why. After that the cooperation between our two companies dwindled and then completely disappeared. To this day I cannot forgive my board their ostrich mentality.

The second foray abroad was when Jock Hamilton mooted the idea of an air safari venture in England – catering for charter flights for travel-loving English. Meredith, Snelgar and Gratz went in for the venture. The General and I declined. I did not wish to invest in a concern so far afield as the UK, and one in which I would have no control, relying on spasmodic reports. We were proved right. After flourishing for the first two years, greed got the better of Jock's air safaris – they acquired more and more small aircraft for their charters, eventually overcapitalising. A lull in the tourist market caught them, and Air Safaris Ltd was liquidated. My mates had to dig deep into their pockets, while I tried not to gloat. The air business is ever a bucking bronco – so easy to fall, and so hard. I felt sorry for Jock – even a cautious Scot can be thrown.

Trek/Luxavia Philosophy

Throughout our aviation adventures, our board always maintained one guiding principle. Cobbler stick to your last, i.e. stick to your own profession. Many times we were tempted, sorely tempted, to venture further afield – to explore beyond the African continent or to compete on the local routes – even to spend our reserves on more modern, more up-to-date planes – to try other avenues for profit. Luckily, we resisted. True, on one occasion we did take a share in the new hotel which Luxembourg was erecting at their new airport. But the outlay was moderate and our main motive was to build goodwill in our new home country. Other than this, we adopted a blinkered approach to change. We avoided extraneous pitfalls, and like the weary ploughman we wended our way ploddingly forward. It paid off.

Safmarine

After some years of happy and profitable association with Joggie and his Rentmeester Beleggings, at our usual Friday meeting Joggie made a proposal. He said that an approach had been made to him by Safmarine, a quoted company conducting a highly rated travel business, mostly marine. They wished to diversify into the air – would Luxavia consider a minor investment (not a takeover)? They were a well-conducted, successful concern, with the ear and full support of the government. Joggie urged us to consider very seriously offering them a 25% interest at a price that was favourable to us. We had by now been battling (albeit with much profit) for a quarter of a century. Surely the time had come to consolidate our personal lives! We parted with our shares, which left us with only 50%, the other 50% being held by Rentmeester and Safmarine. At least we were safe, and our future was secured. Grudges there were, but caution and prudence triumphed.

The years rolled on, and I still remained in the chair. The presence of two reputable chairmen of two important JSE-quoted companies on our board did not overawe. We all worked well and harmoniously together, with no problems worth mentioning. But flying for me had become monotonous – simply a jet rush to get there – no night-stops, no thrills, very little of interest in the air. The ups and downs of the early Trek era were no longer there. We had as many flights scheduled as we could comfortably handle, our planes were all that we desired. But there was no longer incentive for change and progress. I was bored.

Just after Trek/Lux's thirtieth birthday, Jock said it was time for him to retire to the farm which he had bought in the south of England – Ashley Clinton Manor – a gentleman's residence.

Ashley Clinton Manor was the ruined home of General Sir Henry Clinton, who had led the British forces against Washington in the American War of Independence. It was now certainly a gentleman's residence – the address being Ashley Clinton Manor,

Lymington Road, New Milton, Hants (Jock recounted a story of how shortly after he and his family had moved into their new home, his wife Doris had purchased some goods which had to be delivered. The shop assistant, on being given the address, replied, 'Certainly, Lady Hamilton.' This always amused our pretentious Jock).

Safmarine made him a good offer for his shares. When I heard the price I remarked not too earnestly, 'If they want my shares at that price they can have them.' They wanted. A while back General von Mellenthin had been coaxed away to become Lufthansa's SA commercial manager – a position which he could hardly refuse. Cecil Snelgar and Fred Gratz likewise offered their shareholdings. Overnight we all four went on pension – only Tom remained, because they offered him the managing director's post (CEO) – a job that he had for years been pestering us to give him. No dice – we still remembered the Fanie Botha incident. We were out and Tom was happy. He was at last 'the captain'. Good luck to him.

It was a wrench, but we at least had our odd complimentary flights when the spirit urged – which it did not do very often. To rush over in one day to Europe, and land at Luxembourg or Heathrow as an ordinary passenger, with no VIP treatment, did not really appeal. Having no business to attend to on arrival, and having no longer any connections with the busy world of commerce made the whole trip an anticlimax. I had been spoilt.

The Demise

However, aviation was still in our blood, and all the retirees avidly followed Lux's expansion. More expensive aircraft were apparently laid on at the drop of a hat – not paid for in cash, as was our principle, but no doubt on the never-never system. Flights were organised on all sorts of routes that we had avoided. Then came the great development – Trek Airways was revived, but under a new name, Flitestar, to operate on all the local routes in direct opposition to SAA and all the other carriers – another expansion that we had scrupulously avoided. For a time, we outsiders envied the new set-up – it seemed to make our old operation so puny. Then a great tragedy occurred – Joggie, returning in a small aircraft charter flight to Nelspruit, took off in bad weather, crashed and was killed. We all attended his funeral, and agreed that we had lost a good and true man and friend. Each one of us had a catch in our throat. Joggie Vermooten was no more.

How this affected the running of Trek/Lux I never knew. But what we did know was that the local press one day had headlines announcing that today's flight of Flitestar would be the last. The company was insolvent and was followed by Luxavia into liquidation. We all cried – the end of an era. Just prior to his death, which came not long after, Tom Meredith made a very sage remark. 'What we built up in thirty years they broke down in ten.'

Today the General, Cecil Snelgar, Fred Gratz and my close friend Jock Hamilton are all gone for ever, as also Syd Excel and Fanie Botha – only I of the four musketeers have been spared to chronicle those hectic Trek days of the fifties in the year of our Lord 2002.

As I motored along the M1 to my farewell party in Johannesburg I passed the names of Ben Schoeman and Danie Joubert and my mind went back to these two gentlemen who had had so much to do with Trek.

I remembered them not without a measure of affection, because although the majority of our shareholders were not of their political persuasion, they had always treated us fairly. What more could we ask? Then followed a wave of nostalgia. I began to recall the good and the bad days in our history. Only two really bad events came to mind.

The first was when Cecil Snelgar, while warming up his engines at dawn take-off from Entebbe, was horrified to see an innocent local walking carelessly into a propeller. He was instantly beheaded. Cecil, although completely blameless, was arrested, and Trek had to bail him out. The case was only heard many months later, after an anxious waiting period. One never knows how central African justice will be meted out. Luckily Cecil was discharged – he breathed a sigh of great relief.

The second, more serious incident occurred just after Tom Meredith took off early in the morning from Cairo. Hardly airborne, with horror he saw smoke pouring out of the starboard engine. The fire was spreading, and the extinguishers were ineffective. Tom made an excellent crash landing on the sands of the Sahara, not far from the airport. The pax were unharmed, and were eventually ferried back to Jan Smuts on a relief Trek aircraft. A terrifying experience, which we suspected was due to sabotage against South Africa, but we could say nothing – our insurance might not pay if sabotage could be proved. After some months of haggling with our insurers in London, Lloyds paid us a cheque for £75,000 for our lost DC-4. As Lloyds rather reluctantly settled our brokers, Norman Frizzel in London suggested that I should become a 'name' at Lloyds. For £25,000 I would have a 'safe' lifetime investment. To be a 'name' in London is considered prestigious, as it is only by invitation. I was tempted, as the money was now available, but what held me back was the unlimited liability clause. I considered it a dangerous risk, despite their absolute assurance that Lloyds was as safe as the Bank of England. Thank goodness I was cautious, because many years later my friends in England had to face enormous financial losses when Lloyds held them to the unlimited liability clause. Wealthy men had to sell up their homes. I was lucky – sometimes I am, not always.

After these dismal reflections as I drove, I thought back to some of Trek's lighter moments.

Before we had tied up our Lux agreement and Luxavia was born, sanctions forced Trek to abandon the usual routes of direct overflying of central African states, who had banned SA aircraft. We pioneered the West Coast route over Luanda, a route that no airline had before flown. On one such flight our crew was forced to land for refuelling at El Golea, in the West African desert. Tragedy – the caravan crossing the desert with the fuel had been waylaid by bandits. The storage tanks were empty and it would be days before fresh supplies arrived. Our captain was desperate. Where would some thirty odd pax spend the night in the desert? Suddenly an Air France airliner landed. Our skipper asked them please to help us out by siphoning enough fuel to get us back to civilisation. The French commander spoke no English, but eventually cottoned on. He glanced approvingly at one of our pretty hostesses, a redhead. 'I give but first I must sleep with the redhead.' We got our fuel, but whether it cost our hostess her virginity we never found out. In any case, was there ever a virginal air hostess?

Nearing our Johannesburg office, I also recalled some of the lighter moments in our Friday meetings with Tom Meredith, who despite always being most conscious of his title 'Captain', also had a whimsical, cockney sense of humour. Sometimes he would blurt without any finesse, 'It will be in all the papers tomorrow.' When someone said, 'What will be in the papers?' he would laughingly reply, 'Fish and chips, of course.' On another occasion, he said before I opened the meeting that he had something to report. Gravely he announced, 'The hostesses have gone on strike. They are dissatisfied with their working conditions.' The meeting was aghast, as we had only recently given them generous pay rises. Then came Tom's bawdy reply: 'They want shorter periods and longer routes.' Collapse of the board.

I drove sadly back from the farewell party, a nostalgic affair. For me, Trek was now dead. Thirty years of mixed experiences, some good, some bad – but always challenging, always exhilarating. Thirty wonderful years!

It was with tremendous shock that I read in the *Pretoria News* of Trek's downfall – the same newspaper that some forty years back had announced that Sydney Excel had been arrested for attempted murder. So much had happened since then.

The images ran through my thinking – Sydney Excel, Fanie Botha, Charles Patmore and all our confrontations with the NTC and with Ben Schoeman. A flood of memories.

In a lifetime of surprises, perhaps the most unexpected occurred on the day of the coronation of Queen Elizabeth of England in 1953. Trek had not yet begun, and I had only recently met Fanie Botha, and knew nothing of him except that he was an important Broederbonder and Mayor of Heidelberg.

Yes, Fanie Botha was a closed book to me when he walked into my office in Pretoria that day and asked if I would favour him by despatching two overseas cables, for which he would of course pay. Naturally I agreed, but to whom? His reply staggered me. 'To the Queen of England – one from me as Mayor and one from me personally.'

'But,' said I, 'how can you personally address royalty, the Queen?'

'Because,' he replied, 'I know her very well. When she was a small girl I used to rock her on my knee.' I thought he was pulling my leg, but then his naval history in England came out – his visits to Scotland with the Duke of York. I personally sent off the two cables – so I knew they were genuine. Fanie then told me how he again met the royal family during their 1947 visit to South Africa. He was busy with his famous 'Huggins' Folly' in Rhodesia. One afternoon he wanted to cross the Victoria Falls Bridge to get home. Guards would not let him pass, as the royal family was in residence in the royal train nearby. He persuaded the chief guard to take a note to the King, which after much haggling he reluctantly agreed to do. 'Shorty Botha wants to cross the bridge. Has he your Majesty's permission to do so?' Back came the reply: 'Permission granted, provided you come in and see us. George R.' Fanie still had that note and produced it from his wallet to show me. He spent a pleasant hour with the family – the last time that he ever saw them.

This incident convinced me that Fanie's subsequent tales of his overseas adventures in America, Australia and the UK were not fabrication. Just as Syd Excel's testimony under oath in his murder trial verified his army escapades.

Fanie Botha and Sydney Excel were two exceptional but bizarre characters. Both of them unusually affable and likeable, but sometimes unbearably self-opinionated and even vicious. But without both of them there would have been no Trek Airways. Out of the strong comes forth sweetness.

On that fateful day I looked again at the article announcing Trek's demise in the *Pretoria News* – I thought back when that same daily had announced to the world that Sydney Excel had been arrested for attempted murder – just forty years ago.

It was then that I found myself wistfully humming the words, which so many years ago we had always sung on school-leaving day:

> 'Forty years on when afar and asunder
> Departed are those who are singing today
> Then you may look back and forgetfully wonder
> What you were like in your work and your play.'

Forty years come and forty years gone – and no more Trek, nor ever would there again be in the history of aviation. The world was careering at too breakneck a pace.

More's the pity.

The Years After

The years have come, the years have gone – nothing remains but solitude.

There is now time to sit back and to cherish memories of times that were, times that could have been, and times that may still be.

It is with gratitude that I recall those who goaded me so persistently to join their pipe dream. Now I can reflect on what rewards their enterprise brought into our lives and those around us – magnificent, unsought for and unexpected rewards! And what happiness it provided in the lives of so many throughout the length and breadth of our beloved South Africa who were passengers to lands far beyond our shores – not to mention the hundreds of immigrants who made their homes here and learned to enjoy the warm sunshine and friendly hospitality of our land.

These memories are ample compensation for all our thirty years of blood, sweat and tears, full of anxieties, hopes, setbacks. But at last we have earned the fulfilment of those early dreams of so long ago, and are quite content to take our rest and hand over our heritage to others – others who, alas, in a few short years undid what we had built so carefully over so many years. A great sadness!

Now in comfort can I look back and savour fond memories, but like the sundial I record only the sunny hours.

The Aircraft

Well do I recall that first Dakota, the beloved DC-3 that Fred Gratz so diligently and so expertly built up from the hull that survived the second great war. With disappointment I remember the perfidy of Fanie Botha in selling our only asset, but with admiration I reflect on the promptitude with which Jock Hamilton delivered to us those three small Vikings, which were to serve us so faithfully for so many years.

Each seated only twenty-eight passengers within its delicate frame supported by only fabric wings and two propellers. Delicate was each and, by today's standards, flimsy. But each had a metaphorical heart as stout as bold Cortez of yore, standing upon a peak in Darien. Nobly and faithfully did they serve us, until the National Transport Commission gave permission for us to graduate to four engines over Africa – the Douglas DC-4 Skymaster.

Thanks to the unremitting maintenance schedules of Gratz and his expert gang of engineers, only once did a Viking cause us concern. It was on the final leg of a southbound flight when over the great, grey, greasy Limpopo River, an errant eagle flew slap bang through the fabric of the starboard wing. An immediate forced landing was imperative. Luckily Pietersburg Airport was at hand, and luckily our ace number one Commander Cornie Balt in control. With his usual aplomb Cornie calmly announced an unscheduled stop for a meal and to enable pax to freshen up for the Jan Smuts landing. Applause! Not a word about the mishap! After a pleasant interlude on the ground, the pax, well fed, were transferred to a standby Viking that had been hurriedly rustled up from Jan Smuts within the hour. Not a single passenger was aware of the flimsy fabric wing – it remained a company secret until this confession of mine today. In any air service public confidence is paramount, as was so bitterly realised after the New York disaster of 11 September 2001. Fortune does not always favour the brave.

The gentle Vikings had to be tended with devotion, handled with care. The delicacy of their structure was never a hazard, provided that one respected their maximum overall carrying capacity. To us who had suffered the overloading problem of Phoenix Airlines the message was loud and clear. Always, but always respect the weight factor! (As every blonde bombshell of today so fervently realises!)

In the rarefied atmosphere of Jan Smuts Airport (Johannesburg International today), more fuel was required than at sea level. Therefore overall weight must be restricted to allow for a larger intake of fuel. Each passenger together with his or her baggage had to be carefully weighed after refuelling, and a meticulous calculation made to determine what overall weight of pax was permissible to keep within the maximum overall weight limit. If all twenty-eight passengers were of average stature and build there would normally be room for one or perhaps two supernumeraries aboard – complimentary or staff members.

I was in the habit of spending one month each year inspecting the overseas offices. July was the chosen month, as I was then on holiday from my lectures at Pretoria University. Furthermore, my beloved London was agog with sport. For twenty-five years I never missed July in Europe. The snag was that this was the heart of the summer season overseas, and all flights were completely booked out. My complimentary seat depended upon the overall weight of the Viking flight. Normally the crew managed to keep a seat for me, but I remember one occasion when I missed out. I stood, baggage in hand, watching the weighing in. Three passengers were still to arrive and it seemed that my seat was secure. They arrived, three Orange Free State farmers – jovial, but enormous, as gigantic as only a Free State farmer can be from his diet of meat at every meal on plates the size of manhole covers. I had to wait for the next flight.

In this respect South African Airways was always very kind to me – I had only to request a first-class complimentary booking and they would invariably grant it. But this facility I rarely exercised – only when time was of the essence to meet some urgent deadline. In my book no one-day flight of South African Airways, first class though it might be, could ever compare with the enjoyment of the four leisurely days over Africa with three night-stops in exotic lands and magnificent hotels. Supreme luxury.

When the National Transport Commission so grudgingly permitted Trek to graduate to four-engined aircraft, we bade a sad though grateful farewell to our small Vikings, but breathed a sigh of relief as we at last had four engines over Africa.

In the early days John Foggitt used to fill our southbound flights with immigrants from Europe – young men fleeing from the deprivations of post-war Europe in search of a new life far from the desolated and bombed zones of the last great war. The whole rehabilitation scheme of Samorgan was executed with such ruthless efficiency as only one with John Foggitt's expertise could command.

Invariably these young adventure-seekers would, for the first two days of the flight, sit silently in their seats, no doubt brooding over the home hearths that they were leaving far behind. Gradually they would make friends aboard, and start standing around in groups, chatting in many different tongues. One such group gravitated to the rear of the plane, and eventually started dancing in the aisle. This was too much for the balance of the sensitive Viking, and its tail began to droop. Politely, but firmly, came the command from the cockpit for passengers to resume their seats. An illustration of the vigilance that was required even in the air to distribute the load evenly, so as to avoid imbalance. Yes, we had to pamper our Vikings always! And always did they respond!

Only when at last the National Transport Commission grudgingly allowed us to graduate to larger aircraft carrying more passengers, did these weight nightmares subside.

As we bade a sad farewell to pension off our three Vikings, we could at last breathe more freely with our new DC-4, with two extra engines, over the wilds of Africa. For years we had constantly held thumbs that no Viking engine would fail aloft over the jungles in Africa and cause us to do a forced landing in a forest or a desert – a prospect to be contemplated only with fearful trepidation. Praise be, it never happened – someone above was looking after us!

That trusty warhorse, the sixty-seater Skymaster DC-4, allayed our fears of engine failure, but now we had no aircraft in reserve in case of emergency. The National Transport Commission, egged on by a rapacious South African Airways, would allow us not one extra seat to sell – certainly no second aircraft. Not a week would pass without our new baby being in service. There was no rest for the Skymaster! Fred Gratz's workshop had perforce to work overtime each weekend to keep the service schedule up to date, a great job they did! We knew that the time would surely come when one engine might need replacements en route. With this in mind, we stationed spare engines at certain night-stops, ready for any emergency.

We had always shuddered to think what might have happened had that errant eagle crashed through the plane wing over the wilds of central Africa or the Western Desert of North Africa. Without complete conviction we liked to believe that Cornie Balt would have had the skill to land without disaster – but we thanked the gods that his airmanship was never put to such a test!

With our newly acquired four-engined DC-4 we slept more restfully at night. But we also realised that now we had no backup aircraft should an emergency arise. Fred Gratz arranged for spare engines to be located at all the night-stops along the route, so that any faulty motor could be replaced without delay in transit.

Only once did an emergency arise – during the final leg of a northbound flight over the snow-covered Swiss Alps. A port engine ceased to function. I happened to be on board, and at last could realise that a silent propeller in flight could be just as frightening as a V2 bomb over London in wartime. Again it was Cornie Balt in the left-hand seat, so I was not unduly perturbed. Nevertheless, it was with relief that we safely landed at Düsseldorf. Our spare engine was in Hamburg, so after allowing the passengers to disembark, the aircrew flew on to that north Germany port. I decided to accompany them, not being regarded as a passenger – because no take-off on less than four engines was permitted with any pax aboard. I wanted the experience, but also did not wish the aircrews to think of their chairman as being afraid of risks – and a risk it would be if the other port motor should also decide to malfunction. The operation went off smoothly, and after two days in Hamburg we returned safely to Düsseldorf with all four propellers in action. This was the nearest that Trek ever came to a forced landing with our trusty Skymaster, which served us faithfully until the crash of South African Airways enabled Trek at last to graduate to jets.

It was in the 1960s that hijacking of aircraft became the vogue – either for political or financial gain. Trek was fortunate in managing to arrange cover with Lloyds against such destructive acts.

In July 1965 I was in the Düsseldorf office awaiting a southbound flight in two days' time. A mysterious telephone call was received anonymously from a so-called benefactor of Trek, warning that the very next flight was going to be hijacked over the Mediterranean and held ransom for one million pounds.

I would be aboard. The seizure of our aircraft for the ransom did not perturb us particularly – Lloyds had covered us. But holding the chairman of the company hostage was another matter. For Trek this would be serious and expensive – and for me personally it was mind-boggling and terrifying! I feverishly goaded the office staff into action, working through the night for the next two days. We followed a carefully devised plan. The passenger list was analysed in great detail, assessing the possibility of each passenger being a hijacker. First we discarded all returning passengers whose tickets had been purchased months ago in South Africa. The aircraft seizure was unlikely to have been planned so far in advance. Persons accompanied by children were also disregarded – who would endanger the life of their offspring? Each one of the remaining pax was closely scrutinised. Four with home addresses in the Middle East were transferred to flights on other airlines – 'Sorry, we had made a double-booking – our apologies!' We then set about tracing the history of every remaining passenger. We contacted agents who had done the booking or telephoned home addresses where these were available. Eventually we narrowed the suspect list, and instructed our airport staff to conduct thorough body checks on each suspect before boarding. No more could we do.

On the morning of take-off we were jittery – particularly me, with fear in the pit of my stomach – but life must go on! Two passengers of doubtful appearance were shunted off to other airlines, with our abject apologies.

As we took off I seated myself in the front seat just before the door to the cockpit, which was locked throughout the flight. It was only over the Mediterranean that I experienced a scare. A man in a long blue mackintosh rose from a back seat and walked up the aisle towards the cockpit. This is it, thought I! I met him halfway and asked if I could assist him in any way. After talking for some ten minutes I was convinced that he meant no harm. What a relief!

Only on the third day out did I begin to relax. I asked a hostess for a neat double whisky, which she served to me wide-eyed, as it was well known that normally my alcohol intake aboard was only a light sherry with meals. At times circumstances make fools of the best of us! Without mishap on the fourth day we landed safely at Jan Smuts. None of the passengers had had an inkling of the impending threat or how relieved the crew was – particularly the chairman!

It might have been a coincidence, but on the very next southbound flight just after take-off from Cairo, a flame issued from a starboard engine. The fire extinguishers had no effect, and the flame burnt unusually blue. The commander had no option but to make a forced landing on the sands of the Western Desert – which he did with commendable expertise. No one was injured, and it was not long before buses brought the pax back to the Nile Hilton Hotel, where they enjoyed an extra day's leave awaiting the arrival of an Irish plane that we were forced to charter to fly back to Jan Smuts. On arrival home we presented each passenger with a handsome bouquet of flowers, as our token of apology for the delay. For most of them, I am sure, it was but an extra holiday.

The insurance claim was not so straightforward. I was forced to fly to Lloyds to assure them that the accident was through no fault of ours, and to deny that it was a hijacking attempt. I was relieved when I eventually pocketed the cheque for £75,000.

It was the last hiccup that we had with our propeller-driven aircraft, but it was still a relief when many years later we were authorised to swap the piston for the jet. Thereafter hitches were slight and unimportant. For which Allah be praised!

The Passengers

Over the years many and varied were the types of passengers who booked with Trek, especially after a few years when the quality of our service on board and the reliability of our flights began to be appreciated by the public in general. Persons of high social standing were attracted to us, as were the lowly immigrants who were forced to use us for economic reasons.

In the early days of our Vikings, because of air pressurisation we could not cruise at high altitudes. At 8,000 feet there was sometimes turbulence, especially in descent. One incident comes to mind.

It was when Samorgan was bringing loads of young German post-war immigrants to the developing Orange Free State mines. My wife was on board when the full complement of pax consisted of 24-year-old immigrants escaping from the aftermath of the war in Germany.

They were seeking a new life abroad. Ticatic (my wife), returning from holiday, was obliged to act as the sole hostess, as illness had overtaken the usual crew. The majority of these young Germans had, I am sure, only seen aircraft when they were dropping bombs on them out of the skies. Hapless and already homesick most of them were, and scared out of their wits. Soon after being airborne they began one after the other to resort to the airsick bags. By the time of their first landing in Malta the stench disgusted my wife. Before take-off the next morning after the night-stop, Ticatic asked permission from the captain to address the seated pax. This she did in no uncertain manner as was her wont, with no mincing of words – 'Control yourselves, and if I see anyone reaching for a sick bag I shall personally deal with him,' she roared. They were too petrified of her to disobey, so the stench never again occurred.

It was with smiling faces that the young men disembarked at Cairo for the second night-stop in the luxurious Nile Hilton

Hotel – such an edifice as they had probably never before seen. Nor had they ever seen the glittering array of silver cutlery which confronted them at the dinner table that night. They were completely confused by all the tableware before them. As it happened, my wife's first-born, fifteen-year-old son, Bokkie, was also aboard. With his mischievous sense of humour, Bokkie saw their bewilderment and would purposely pick up the wrong implement. Everyone would automatically follow him, whereupon he would quickly resort to the right utensil, with a deadpan expression. An amusing but heartless prank, to which my wife soon put a stop. It served to illustrate how deprived those youths of Germany were through years of relentless war. I often wonder what has become of all that army of Samorgan's immigrants who settled beneath our sunny skies. Hopefully many of them have found happiness and prosperity in our fair land.

Another amusing incident happened to two complimentary passengers – my wife Ticatic and our director, General Helm von Mellenthin. They were both on the same flight some time later, also night-stopping in Cairo. In those days health authorities were very strict about medical injections both for smallpox and yellow fever. Ticatic and Helm had both had their injections, but not quite ten days before landing in Egypt, as was the requirement. Both were therefore shunted off in front of all the other passengers by the Cairo health inspectors.

They were sent to a local prison camp for the night. All their protests fell on deaf ears. No Nile Hilton Hotel for them! Both were furious, but to no avail. Helm in particular must have been angrily vociferous – he who had in Nazi uniform looked down on all Egyptians during Hitler's North African campaign, was now to be snubbed by them. Each had to spend the night in a bedroom facing a long veranda. It was stiflingly hot, as only Cairo can be in summer. They asked permission to take their beds out of the stuffy room onto the veranda. The guards could not understand English, try as hard as Helm did to communicate with them. At last a more literate guard arrived, but his understanding of English was most limited. Eventually he said to the General: 'Oh, I see, you want to sleep with the lady.' Helm collapsed and gave up the struggle. Both were relieved in the morning again to join the other pax who had spent a memorable night in the magnificent Nile Hilton Hotel – but rather shamefaced, neither ever again delayed the medical injections.

We were sometimes saddled with eccentric passengers. One such person I myself had persuaded to fly Trek. She was the wife of a Swiss caterer who had immigrated to South Africa and opened up a flourishing restaurant in Pretoria – 'Janina'. I was their auditor, and so had much contact with the wife, Mrs Brandli, who kept the books.

After I convinced her to fly Trek for her homeward holiday, I felt it my duty to wave her off from the tarmac at Jan Smuts Airport.

It was only when the hostess on this flight returned to South Africa that I learned of Mrs Brandli's bizarre behaviour on board. Apparently on the last day, as the plane took off from Malta, she locked herself in one of the toilets and refused to come out until landing in Zürich, which was still hours away. Her excuse was that someone was following her – in fact, she claimed he was looking at her from outside the window of the loo. As one passenger facetiously remarked, 'It must be the angel Gabriel.' No amount of persuasion could change her mind, to the annoyance of the other pax who wished to freshen up for the landing – since it meant there was one toilet less! Only when the engines came to rest in Zürich did she emerge at the appearance of a hastily summoned Swiss doctor, who rushed her to a local sanatorium; she was consequently reported to have recovered from her mental aberration.

She enjoyed her holiday in her hometown. On her return she was perfectly normal and never was the subject discussed between us – tact was the order of the day.

What a mystery the human brain is!

Loath as I am to make light of matters of a lavatorial nature, I feel constrained to relate another experience in one of Trek's loos. The passenger was of an unusual size – to be blunt, she was grossly obese with fatty tissue oozing from every corner. Possibly the wife of another Orange Free State farmer! She ensconced herself on the seat of the loo, but found herself unable to rise. Her surplus flesh had overflowed the seat and formed a vacuum which her legs were unable to break. She was stuck! Her shouts attracted a hostess who opened the door, but she could not shift the huge body either. Tongue in cheek, the hostess called for the flight engineer who arrived post-haste with spanner in hand, thinking it was a toilet repair. Suppressing his smiles, the quick-thinking technician, to the embarrassment of both, set to work and managed to break the vacuum. How he achieved this is today still a closely guarded secret – a task worthy of Hercules. Only with effort did the rest of the passengers aboard manage to keep their mirth below the surface. Discretion was always an indispensable attribute of the Trek Airways staff – the better part of valour.

A third loo episode also occurred on a certain northbound flight. A couple was by chance seated together, although obviously travelling separately. After three days of conversing, on the last day of the flight a hostess noticed an unmistakable intimacy becoming manifest. She was not surprised when some time later they arose and both went together into the same loo.

Again the discretion which was always inculcated into Trek's crew came to the fore, and the hostess did not feel constrained to mention that joint use of the lavatory was not permitted. It was half an hour before they emerged, and from their contented expressions, she could only conclude that they had contrived to join the mile-high club. But whether they completed the whole course or reached just 880 yards, she could only speculate. With a twinkle in her eye however, the fun-loving hostess, bearing in mind that the incident took place over the sands of the great Sahara Desert quoted the rhyme about the sands of the Nile, whose blockage accounted for the hump on the camel and the Sphinx's inscrutable smile – naughty!

On another flight we carried a honeymoon couple. For years they had been pen friends, but had never actually met. The groom had recently flown out from his native United States, at last met his South African bride, married her the day before the flight, and they were now hurrying back to New York via Europe.

The first night-stop was in Uganda at a little-used airstrip near Kampala. Our Trek plane was the largest aircraft that had ever landed there. The local tribe was fascinated by its size, and they gathered round, clad only in their tribal dress, gazing in amazement at this large bird.

They were of the tribe whose cult it was to attach stones to their equipment so as to increase its length. As a result their private parts hung down to their knees, in full view of everyone. The Trek passengers disembarked and were standing round waiting to be transported to the hotel. After a few minutes the American approached our captain and asked whether we could move on.

The skipper laughingly asked him whether his new wife was embarrassed. 'Oh no,' replied the passenger, 'but I don't want her to think tonight that I am malformed.'

Collapse of the captain.

It was several years later that I was told some further strange customs of the Kikuyu, a people of East Africa dwelling in the highlands west of Mount Kenya. It was known as Kikuyuland near Entebe, Nairobi.

These are some of the things that I heard.

The Kikuyu have a medicine man or woman, who is expected to shave their head completely. A medicine woman wears loops of beads on either side of the head. Usually she wears a leather dress, lots of beaded necklaces across her breasts and shoulders. Lots of beads and copper bangles are worn on the arms and legs. Quite often copper head bands are worn as well.

At the beginning of the twentieth century the tribe was still very primitive. For example, they never wore shoes. When eating, they used only their hands – they had no such thing as a knife and fork. Most men and women couldn't read or write.

Their views and notions of pain and death were completely different to those of European civilisations. From birth, children were taught not to show weakness; they accepted famine, sickness and death as the will of God – that is, their god, Ngai. He lived on Mount Kenya. They believed that it was he who had created the world.

It was accepted that a girl in childhood must undergo ear piercing. Usually the first two holes were made through the sensitive cartilage in the tops of the ears. At a later stage, as the girl approached adulthood, the larger bottom hole was created. Usually the young woman had to lie flat on the ground, and then the medicine man or woman used sharpened sticks to pierce her ears. These sticks were kept in place for about three weeks. This would be extremely painful for the young girl and she would find it difficult to lie down. During this time a young girl would find sleeping near impossible as the sticks were uncomfortable. What a relief when the wounds were healed and the sticks could be removed. The ears were then smeared with a healing salve (from local plants) on the scabs. When the ears were completely healed, they were ready for the rings of copper beads that were worn according to Kikuyu custom.

This piercing of the ears is almost trivial compared to the ancient initiation of circumcision for all girls between the ages of nine and seventeen.

The ceremonial surgery was called *irua*. The young girl initiates would be required to bathe naked, up to their breasts in icy water of a nearby river. The idea was to make the area numb, as no anaesthetic would be used in the following ritual. Hence the young girls stayed in the freezing water until they had little or no feeling below the waist. They would now be ready for the next step in the initiation. There were three steps which had to be taken. Firstly there was the removal of the clitoris, then the trimming of the labia and lastly the suturing shut of the vulva. A surgical razor was used to perform these operations. The purpose of this was to discourage lust in girls, to curb sexual promiscuity and to make masturbation impossible. With the sensitive part of the genitals cut away, as well as the vaginal opening being reduced to about the width of a little finger, it was believed that this would discourage girls from experimenting before marriage. The girls were expected to lie on the ground that had been prepared for the initiation. They would bend their arms at their elbows and press the elbows into the ribs, their hands raised – they could make their hands into fists, with their thumbs inserted between the first and second fingers to indicate that they were ready to commence the next step of their initiation. After the 'operation', soothing herbs and various plants were crushed together. This was applied to the wounds. Finally, sweet smelling leaves were bound between the girls' legs. (Apparently the herbs and the leaves used were passed down to each generation.)

Later each girl before she got married would have to undergo an examination to establish that the future bride was indeed a virgin. It was the duty of the medicine man/woman to then make the necessary incision to enable intercourse to take place after her marriage.

This mutilation of a girl's sexual organs often resulted in very difficult births and quite often as a result women would die in childbirth. When the missionaries came to Africa they tried to abolish this practice, but they met with strong opposition as after all the custom had been in existence for hundreds of years. The Kikuyu considered the process of initiation into womanhood sacred and holy. They did not consider it to be cruel and inhuman. The fact that very often blood poisoning occurred was overlooked. After all, it was a tribal custom that had to be adhered to.

Another example of Trek's discretion was when pax were being allotted rooms for the first night-stop in the Lake Victoria Hotel on the banks of Africa's largest lake.

Peter Urquhart, the radio operator, was entrusted with the task. Peter was possessed with a twinkling eye and a delightful sense of humour. A young man escorting an attractive girl, whom he had obviously just met on that first day of the flight, asked confidentially whether they could be put into adjoining rooms. Quick as a flash came back Peter's reply – 'I'll put you together in a double room if you wish.' The English passenger blushed and blurted out, 'I say, old man, that's frightfully sporting of you.' Trek aims to please! The Englishman was not a mile-high club candidate, but not far from falling into that category.

This incident seems to endorse the dictum of Trek Airways aircrews, who averred that when a lady flew alone, as the plane passed northbound across the Limpopo River she would quietly pluck her wedding ring from her finger and hide it deep in her handbag for the rest of the flight – perhaps even far beyond this.

No wonder a wag once altered one of Trek's advertising slogans by deleting the first two letters of the final word: 'Trek's flights are filled with glamour' to 'Trek's flights are filled with amour.'

Had Shakespeare lived in today's world he might well have

amended his dissertation on music to read: 'If flying be the food of love, fly on.'

Another of Trek's unusual passengers came to me from a good friend of mine, Dr Horace Berliner. But then Horace was himself an unusual person! Firstly, he had a double doctorate in Engineering, and secondly he had an Athletic Blue. He spent some years at Oxford University in the mid-1930s, where, not content with being capped as a Doctor of Mechanical Engineering, he stayed on to earn a Civil Engineering Doctorate as well.

It was during his study years that for relaxation he was wont to go down to the athletic field, and leisurely run two or three times round the track in the late afternoon. This is how he came in contact with the varsity team that was preparing for the annual athletic meeting with Cambridge University. He had no pretensions to being an athlete, but was only taking exercise in what was a particularly cold winter in England. When the great day arrived for the contest, he was asked to join the team purely as a pacemaker. It was his function to complete two or three laps at a fast pace in the mile event, then to retire completely exhausted. This was an old ploy of athletes to try and upset the opposition by urging them to over-exhaust themselves.

As the meeting got under way it was bitterly cold with a biting wind. The iciness froze one's legs to the marrow, and caused the leg muscles to go into a state of contraction. But Horace had one unusual advantage – the hairs on his legs were long and thick, and as massive as the covering of the hairiest chimpanzee. Horace in shorts was a sight to behold! But in the inter-varsity mile event it gave him a distinct advantage over the others, whose legs froze and went into spasms – his hairiness protected Horace, who felt no such effects. He completed his two pacemaker laps, then the third lap while he waited for the regular milers to pass him. No one came, so he went on to the last lap – still no arrivals. The upshot was that he was forced to amble round the last lap, and eventually won the event in the record longest-ever time. As winner he had earned his Blue, but it was the first and last time that he ever ran a full mile. In fact, it was his sole appearance ever in any athletic event. But he had his Blue! A bizarre story!

It was in the very early days of Trek that I persuaded Horace and his good wife Jennifer to fly with Trek to Europe on a holiday visit – somewhat reluctantly they agreed, as our flights were still in their infancy and our aircraft was scarily small.

When in London Horace decided to buy his wife a handsome present – a fur coat, very expensive, with some of the money which he had saved on the cheap fare from us. The cost of the fur he could barely afford, and he was certainly in no position to pay British VAT tax over and above, as well as the high import duty which our government would levy on luxury goods at Jan Smuts Airport.

The Berliners therefore devised a plan to escape further taxation. They arranged for the fur to be delivered free of VAT, direct to Heathrow Airport when they were to board a British Airways plane en route to join Trek's Paris departure flight. To hoodwink the customs officers in South Africa they swapped the London labels in the coat for South African labels, which they had brought specially from home in preparation. This would be proof that the coat was a normal item of luggage, no luxury import, meaning no duty to be paid!

Alas, when take-off time at Heathrow arrived, no fur coat had been received. In bitter disappointment they returned without the beloved present.

Back in Pretoria, they begged me to use my position at Trek to help them to import the coat without paying customs duty. Very, very reluctantly I agreed to make a plan during my forthcoming visit to England.

Some weeks later in the London office I found that my return flight would be with a group of young immigrants who had been recruited in England by John Foggitt's Samorgan (before the days of TFC). I called for the passenger list, and found that there was one young lady immigrant booked on the flight. I phoned her in Manchester, asking whether she would be prepared to take a fur coat to South Africa for me. We struck a bargain – she would take delivery of the coat at Heathrow when boarding her link flight to Paris to join the Trek flight. She would also wear it through customs in South Africa, claiming it to be personal baggage. Most important of all, she would hand it back to me after the flight – after all, if she claimed the coat as her own it might be very difficult for me to force legal action against her without admitting complicity to the customs officer which I, in my position as chairman, could not afford to do.

In return I promised her a visit to the famous Lido night-show on the eve of our flight from Paris. I undertook as well to show her the sights of Malta and Luxor in Africa.

A snag arose on the day of departure from London – I still had work to complete in the London office, and would perforce have to take a later flight to the continent. She took delivery of the precious fur at Heathrow as planned. I arranged to meet her later for the first time in the Paris hotel where the passengers were to spend the night at Trek's expense, awaiting the early 6 a.m. departure the next day. So I eventually met Jeannie in Paris – not Jeannie with the light-brown hair, but with a mop of auburn locks. She turned out to be a pleasant enough individual, with a strong English Midlands accent, but quite well educated and intelligent. She was in her early twenties, seeking a new life as an immigrant to South Africa. She had answered an advertisement for a job with Ruto Flour Mills in Pretoria, and I promised to introduce her to her new boss, Reuben Rutowitz, whom I knew as a city councillor in Pretoria.

I met Jeannie that evening as I dined at the Paris hotel with the aircraft crew, and duly fulfilled my commitment to take her to the famous Lido, which I had on previous occasions visited. Jeanie was impressed, as she had never before ventured out of England, and had been somewhat apprehensive about her decision to locate to darkest Africa.

In Malta, where the passengers enjoyed the luxury of the Phoenicia Hotel, we visited the underground caves in which people had sheltered during the wartime German bombing of George Cross Island. Also we saw the world-renowned lace industry in action.

In Luxor, the passengers were charmed by the Tudor-style Winter Palace Hotel. After dinner, we went touring by *garry* to see some of the famous burial sites of the ancient Egyptian pharaohs in the Valley of the Kings – a trip not often undertaken by South African tourists. Jeannie had a special request to make – she had read about the Mohammedan fast of Ramadan, and dearly wanted to see a dance of the dervishes which usually concluded the tour. I managed to persuade a garry to drive the two of us off in search of dervishes, deep in the country area. We arrived at precisely midnight – Ramadan was over, but the dancers were still around in their long white robes. A few piastres persuaded them to give us a repeat performance. A most unique sight!

It was after 3 a.m. that our garry returned us to the Winter Palace Hotel, well satisfied with our evening – after all, how many people are privileged to witness the dance of the dervishes in the month of Ramadan? At the hotel a surprise awaited us. On the large balcony of the hotel overlooking the Valley of the Kings stood a whole complement of Trek passengers, waving at us. What I had not realised was that a northbound Trek flight had also arrived for a night-stop. To avoid congestion at the airport they were scheduled to take off one hour before our time of departure. Consequently they were due for an unusually early four o'clock breakfast with a 5 a.m. take-off. They were now awaiting their breakfast. The aircrew of course recognised me, and it took some explaining to convince them that ours was an innocent journey of adventure – no hanky-panky! I hope they believed me.

In due course the fur coat was safely passed through customs; the Berliners were delighted. I introduced Jeannie to Reuben Rutowitz and the whole affair was settled to everyone's satisfaction.

This anecdote serves to illustrate what privileges were enjoyed by passengers on Trek, and why for so many years so many overseas visitors chose to fly Trek rather than to sit tight for eleven hours in a scheduled aircraft. It was so much more fun, more instructive and definitely much cheaper.

On flights that used Nice instead of Malta as a night-stop, the pax were afforded the opportunity to motor up the mountain road for an evening of gambling at the world-renowned Monte Carlo. This was of course long before South Africa permitted the opening of casinos or the sale of state lottery tickets – an eye-opener for staid South Africans.

On arrival in the early afternoon there would be time for a paddle boat on the blue Mediterranean. Welcome relaxation after a long day's flight over the North African Desert. Real perks for Trek passengers!

What travelling fun the hustle and bustle of jets in the twenty-first century has denied us! No wonder many still hanker after the good old Trek days!

On one flight we carried another interesting passenger – the well-known South African painter, Walter Battiss. Walter, who also lived in Pretoria, was a good friend of mine, but he had not yet achieved his final distinction as a great South African artist. One day he moaned to me that he suffered from the complaint of many an artist – impecuniosity – and he so wanted to attend an art exhibition coming off in London. Trek agreed to give him a complimentary flight in return for a mural to decorate our Johannesburg office. This he duly delivered in the form of a six-foot panel to be attached to the wall of our reception room. Whatever happened to this work of art when Trek folded was a mystery – it should, and possibly did, bring the liquidators a handsome profit. I wonder!

I introduced another Pretoria passenger who was well known and respected. This was George Michael, who was a well-known big game hunter. Not only did he shoot many elephants and lions (sometimes for culling purposes), but he also shot many fascinating photos of African wildlife. His photographic skills took him every year to Hollywood, where he had his own office. George was an attractive personality, with a well-developed sense of humour; he was a great leg-puller.

I recall him telling me that he had many good film-star friends in Hollywood. He was particularly fond of Cary Grant, who apparently had a similarly humorous nature. One day Cary said he was going clay pigeon shooting. George, with a straight face, innocently said, 'What is that?' Cary invited him to come along, and proceeded to demonstrate his shooting ability, hitting first seven out of ten clay pigeons, and then eight out of ten. 'Why don't you try your hand?' said Cary. George promptly shot ten out of ten.

'Very good for a novice,' said Cary. 'Beginner's luck! I bet you a hundred dollars you could not do it again.'

'You're on,' said George and promptly shot another ten.

As he took his hundred dollars, George quietly said, 'I am the reigning South African clay pigeon shooting champion.' What Cary said is not recorded and in any case would probably not be printable.

Trek agreed to give George Michael a complimentary passage provided that he made a film of the entire flight northbound and southbound, with emphasis on the various night-stops. The result was a magnificent record of our flights, which we showed time and time again for advertising purposes. Dearly would I like to know whatever happened to this valuable record.

Trek's Side Issues

For years Trek flights took off regularly twice every week, always on Tuesday and then again on Friday. Our licence stated that officially we were a non-scheduled airline, but as Danie Joubert (he became a good friend of Trek's) once remarked wryly, 'Trek must be the most scheduled non-scheduled operation of world airlines.'

When we had three aircraft we had plenty of capacity to undertake other charter flights. On the African route for years we ran special charters carrying Moslems to Mecca for their annual pilgrimage. We also took religious groups for short tours of Israel, the aircraft waiting to bring the party back after the quick tours of the Holy Land.

Nor did we confine our charter flights to the African continent. Trek often winged its way west and east. To the west on a few occasions we went to South America – 'flying down to Rio'. For passengers wanting a cheap flight to the USA we had a reciprocal agreement with Icelandic Airlines. At Luxembourg the pax would transfer to Icelandic, flying to Kennedy Airport in New York with an intermediate stop in Iceland. It could be arranged to spend two night-stops in Reykjavik, allowing for a quick tour of the island and then catching the next Icelandic flight. Iceland is interesting, particularly to see how hot water is pumped straight into various houses from hot springs in the mountains – who would have thought of such a thing in Iceland, and how many South Africans indeed would normally think of sleeping in Iceland? For the return trip Icelandic had flights taking off from the Bahamas – also very interesting!

We also had many charters to the east, to Bangkok and Hong Kong, sometimes to Mauritius or the Seychelles. To illustrate the excellent value that Trek gave its passengers was a journey of two days Hong Kong, two days aeroplane with excellent hotel accommodation, all for 375 rand. One memorable charter was to

Japan in 1970 to visit the Tokyo Expo, which was an unforgettable experience. The aircraft stayed long enough to enable passengers to ride in the bullet train or to spend some days looking at various exhibits at the expo, to see the huge crowds which attended, normally at least one million persons each day, and particularly to marvel at the fact that each evening as the gates closed there would not be one piece of paper, one plastic bag or even one cigarette stub anywhere to be seen. Compare this with Ellis Park or Wanderers in Johannesburg after a rugby or cricket test match – the ground is like a pigsty. The Japanese are truly a tidy nation!

Charters were arranged often with TFC, or sometimes with other operators or private individuals, but Trek always insisted that our service remain impeccable even when we carried a boisterous crowd of Blue Bull players and fans to play rugby against Wales.

Many South Africans saw many places in the world which they might never have been able to afford without Trek's charter services. Joyous memories!

A feature of every flight was the friendliness of our cabin crews, as well as the facility granted to passengers two by two to visit the cockpit during the long daylight hours of flying, and to learn how the pilots operated the aircraft. Has any other airline offered this opportunity to its pax? I doubt it! What a thrill to be in the cockpit when the plane approached the runway to land at Hong Kong.

Trek's Directors

Fleeting memories of exploits of our directors sometimes come back to me as I in comfort browse over Trek's many happenings.

Sydney Excel

I recall one incident with Syd Excel in the days before we had thought of Trek. He talked me into lending him R700 for a secret project, which he told me would bring to each of us a handsome profit – by next Monday. No more would he say. On the Friday Syd disappeared from his lodgings across the road, and by the next Tuesday had not reappeared. I began to worry, until a telephone call asked me to visit him as he lay in bed in the Pretoria General Hospital. Only then did I learn that he had been in negotiation with a black worker in Premier Diamond Mine (where the Cullinan gem, now in the crown jewels in England, had been found). Syd's contact man had contrived secretly to smuggle out of the mine a large diamond, for which he was demanding R700. Syd could not resist the offer, illegal though it is in South Africa to deal in illicit diamonds. When at the weekend Syd had ridden to a secret rendezvous in the veld to conclude the deal, he had been shot and robbed of his R700. This was his story, which seemed to be confirmed by the gun wound which was being treated in his left side – luckily just missing his heart. Syd recovered, but our stake was lost, and I whistled for my R700. A typical Excel escapade. It should have warned me!

In his frequent ramblings over our sundown cocktails he would casually mention exploits which had occurred during his flights overseas as a pilot for Tropic Airways (before Trek), such as how he had swum the Hellespont, even as Lord Byron had done a century before, or how he had climbed to the top of the Great Pyramid of Giza in less than ten minutes. I had listened to his tales with interest, but also taken them with a pinch of salt.

However, when years later we both happened to be in Egypt on a Trek flight, I dared him for R10 to mount the largest pyramid in ten minutes. It cost me, as his time was only eight minutes. Perhaps there was an element of truth in his other various narrations, told not in a spirit of boastfulness, but in a matter-of-fact tone of voice. His was a character that was difficult to resist.

The General

Another memoir concerns General Helm von Mellenthin. A lasting impression for me was when one day we were both seated together on a flight over the Great Sahara. Helm began to reminisce about his North African campaign as chief of staff to General Rommel in the Western Desert. It was intriguing as he pointed out the remains of crippled tanks still lying abandoned on the desert sands, and described in detail the deployment of his Panzer Divisions leading up to that disaster of Tobruk. How could I ever have imagined during those dark days of Allied defeats in North Africa that I would within ten years be seated with the German chief of staff, being briefed on the strategy that the enemy command had employed during the war? Unbelievable! And how could I have ever thought that between the two of us there would be a bond of friendship engendered by our close association in a joint venture – Trek Airways?

Another side of the General was revealed while we spent a few days in our London office together. Helm asked to join me on the Saturday as I was preparing to visit Lord's for a test match against the West Indies. He wanted to find out more about this English game called cricket. Stoically he sat through the opening overs until the lunch break, sometimes asking questions. As the teams trooped off the field he asked who had won. 'No one has yet won,' I said. 'We shall know by next Tuesday.' He was flabbergasted. 'You mean we have wasted the whole morning?' How could I explain cricket to his German mentality? Quietly he said, 'I think I shall go – I prefer steeplechasing – at least we have a quick result.' He wandered off to explore more exciting sights in London. I still remember General Helm von Mellenthin with nostalgia!

The Years That Might Have Been

As the millennium has now dawned, one sometimes looks back at the twentieth century, with its many, many achievements in all fields of human endeavour – science, medicine, technology, human relations and myriad other matters. But what overshadows all others are the two great wars. What would the world have been without these conflicts!

Certainly without the horrors of Hitler's war and its aftermath, there would have been no Trek umbrella to attract beneath its cover such a conglomeration of men from so many different lands with one common purpose in mind – aviation. Had this not happened, there would have been very different lives for each one of them. It is of interest to speculate how each might have followed his career *sans* war. In my mind's eye I can see how each might have lived his life with not a thought of cruising round God's heaven.

Sydney Excel, in Pretoria in the uniform of a member of the South African police. Fanie Botha, as bottle store owner and Mayor of Heidelberg, still pursuing his eternal quest for his almighty rand, with yet another blonde in tow each week. Rodney Rooken-Smith, still cherishing his big game and conducting overseas safaris to hunt in his beloved Kenya. Helm von Mellenthin, astride his charges in the German cavalry, spending his weekends enjoying his inevitable dressage. Tom Meredith, in the uniform of some constabulary in a far-off English county. Fred Gratz, plying his engineering skills in the South African Air Force at Waterkloof Air Base. Jock Hamilton, eventually qualified as a medico, running a quiet practice in his native Scotland. Paddy Rorke, running his auditing practice in Pretoria and signing balance sheets under the style of W B Rorke and Company. Cecil Snelgar, retired in quiet luxury in his flat in Johannesburg.

Such might have been the pattern of existence for each, but for the interference of that mysterious phenomenon which runs a thread through every country of this world – the unexplained factor acknowledged by all but fathomed by no human brain. The scourge of society, which we in our ignorance, and for want of a better term, call *the finger of fate*.

Jock, in His Own Words (1974)

I was born 2 April 1920 in a small village, Drumsleet, near Dumfries, in south-west Scotland. My parents were poor financially, although my father had made, lost and spent quite considerably before he married at the age of thirty-five (he was fifty when I was born). He had worked his passage to South Africa at the age of seventeen, about the year 1887 or 1888, on a cattle boat, and subsequently worked in the Kimberly diamond mines and the Rand gold mines. He returned to Scotland before the Boer War, then went to Canada, where he worked as a sub-contractor, blasting rocks on the route of the Canadian Pacific Railway to Vancouver. He was reported killed in a rail crash there, but had only been seriously injured. He then returned to Galloway and married my mother, accepting the responsibilities of a family by giving up his adventurous life and settling down to a humdrum job with the London, Midland and Scottish Railway Company until he retired.

I was the youngest of three sons, and was educated at the local village school and at Dumfries Academy (its only previous claim to fame had been that Sir James M Barrie was educated there). I was a mediocre and reluctant student, and at the age of fourteen, I applied to join the RAF as a Boy-Entrant Cadet. I was rejected on medical grounds (heart murmur and severe tonsillitis) and so settled for a job with a firm of accountants. After three years of this, just after the start of the war, I contracted meningitis, followed by acute poisoning of the system caused by overdosage of sulphanilamide tablets, and I was told that I would never be accepted in any of the armed forces.

However, in June 1940 I managed to pass the medical and was accepted into the RAF, but, because of the heart murmur which apparently still persisted, not as a pilot. I chose to become an air-gunner, which involved training as a wireless operator also. Before the aircrew training commenced, I served in various capacities on a balloon barrage site in Glasgow and on ground defence at a fighter station, Warmwell in Dorset. It was there that I first experienced attack by German bombers, both by day and by night, and where I first fired at German aircraft – once from a VGO gun-emplacement in daylight, and once at night using a .303 rifle whilst guarding the hospital. I missed, both times!

After completing aircrew training, I served in Bomber Command, mainly with the RCAF (Royal Canadian Air Force), with 77, 405, 434 and 425 (Alouette) Squadrons. After completion of two tours of operations on Whitleys, Wellingtons and Halifax aircraft, and one term as an instructor at a Heavy Conversion Unit, I joined Transport Command, where I met and crewed with F/O (Flying Officer) Tom Meredith.

We served in West Africa, latterly as VIP crew, flying the GOC (General Office Commanding) West Africa around, then at Kenley and Croydon, flying to Berlin, Athens, Rome, etc., as the forerunners of BBA.

After demob in August 1946, I joined a small charter company at Kenley, British Air Transport, but shortly after, I was asked by Tom Meredith to join him at Liverpool, with a new company named Sky Travel, formed by a carpenter named Stevenson, who wanted us to fly British Wayfarer aircraft to South Africa with immigrants.

The first aircraft was leased from Bristol Aircraft Corporation at a ridiculously small fee, complete with engineer, on the basis that it should be demonstrated in South Africa and in Rhodesia. The first flight left Heathrow Airport about mid-December, 1946, arriving at Rand Airport on 22 or 23 December. This proved to be a rather eventful journey which included being snowed in at Marseilles for about five days.

A second Wayfarer was hire-purchased, and after arrival at Johannesburg in August 1947 with this aircraft, we discovered that the company had been placed in liquidation, and we were stranded. But expenses were regularly sent by the liquidators, and with the help of some freelance flying to Europe we lived fairly comfortably until February 1948, when we flew the aircraft back to the UK to its rightful owners.

During the time in South Africa, we had been approached

several times to charter out the aircraft, thereby earning some money. This was always vetoed by the liquidators, but it gave us our first incentive to form our own operating company.

After collecting six months' salary in the UK, I immediately returned to South Africa, as I had made arrangements to join Pan African Air Charter (PAAC). Some time after that I arranged an appointment with the Cohen & Keyser clan (PAAC) at the William Dempster Airline office in London for Tom Meredith, who was then unemployed, and he subsequently joined me in South Africa.

Pan African Air Charter were at that time operating a great deal to Israel, and we became involved in the first Israeli-Arab war, after the British pulled out of Israel. We received danger money every time we landed at Tel Aviv or Haifa (or at an unnamed military airfield with reinforcements for the Israeli army), because we were shot at indiscriminately by both Arabs and Israelis. Tom was accused of being in league with the Arabs after one flight because he was British and because we had strayed off course in our approach to Israel from Cyprus. PAAC became known as the 'strap-hanger airline' at this time because so many passengers were packed on board.

After I was sacked by PAAC for refusing to cooperate in a currency racket they were operating in Geneva, I joined Universal Air Transport – that was where I met Fred Gratz for the first time. I flew with Mercury Airlines for a short while. It was during this time that I finished up one night in a Paris jail with a badly injured (bitten) nose due to a slight altercation in a Montmartre restaurant with the owner and his waiters over the bill. I was accompanied at the time by W S Haggett, who subsequently became a high executive in the Bristol Aeroplane Company organisation in Canada. He had flown with us on the Bristol Wayfarer. Our other cell companion was a deserter from the French foreign legion. I can't recommend French jail hygiene.

Universal Air Transport was in effect the forerunner of El Al. I spent some time in Israel, flying mainly on the route Tel Aviv–Eilath, which was then a very isolated outpost, heavily guarded by troops, contrasting with its present standing as a holiday resort. At this time I met Cecil Snelgar, who was flying for Suidair International, with Viking aircraft. I also met once again the Australian Don Bennett, who had been my first CO in 77 Squadron. Don ultimately became AVM (Air Vice-Marshal) Bennett, founder of the Pathfinder Force, and Chief Executive of British South American Airways, operating Tudor aircraft to South America. (He was succeeded in the Pathfinder Force by Group Captain Leonard Cheshire VC, with whom I had flown. Leonard subsequently formed the 'Cheshire Homes for the Disabled' throughout the world, after being the British Observer during the American atom bombing of Japan.) Don Bennett was then flying his own Tudor aircraft between Aden and Lydda, carrying Yemenite Jews to their homeland. He told a story of one flight when he arrived at Lydda with one dead elderly Yemenite and one new-born infant on board, with both the death and the birth having occurred during the flight, so at least his passenger number remained accurate.

In 1948, Tom and I formed an air travel and aviation consultancy in equal partnership, known as Meredith and Hamilton, with an office at 204 His Majesty's Building in Johannesburg in South Africa. We instated a female employee to look after the office affairs while we were away flying. I put up the small amount of capital necessary. It was not particularly successful until a contact of Tom's in N'Dota asked us to arrange a charter to take a party of his friends to London and back.

During a brief stay in London between flights, I arranged the charter with 'Crewsair' (whose directors at that time included Barnaby, Keegan and Stevens, who broke away to form BKS Air Transport which is now British Airways north-east, and which caused the downfall of Air Safaris later on.

This confirmed our determination to form our own air company. We considered one or two propositions. We decided to team up with Harry Creed as he said that he had the capital, and the clout with the NTC (we subsequently discovered that he had neither, but we needed a South African national in the company, as Tom was still a British subject).

In 1950 I was very unsettled as to my future. I had aspirations to become a doctor in the UK and had applied to St Bartholomew's Hospital in London, to become a student. However it appeared that there was a three-year waiting list, which made me decide to devote my future to aviation. This was followed by the birth of Tropic Airways (Pty) Ltd. I became a 10% shareholder; Tom a 40% shareholder and Harry Creed 50% (he insisted on having a 50% share). The capital for myself and Tom came from the residue of the Meredith and Hamilton profits and the remainder of my savings. Tropic started with one Dakota (purchased from Africair for about £10,000). Tropic Airways was successful from the start, more by luck than by good judgement. Quite often in the early days, the aircraft left Johannesburg with a northbound load, but had no guarantee of the southbound load. It was strange but something nearly always turned up (as Mr Micawber said). The aircraft was completely paid for after about ten months, and so a decision was taken to purchase the Avro York aircraft which had been used by Field Marshal Jan Smuts. Before this, however, Fred Gratz joined the company as chief engineer. The Dakota was eventually ditched in the Mediterranean between Malta and Benghazi due to engine failure, fortunately without any casualties. This was mainly due to the calmness of the radio officer, the late Peter Urquhart, who alerted rescue organisations and maintained W/T (wireless telegraphy) contact until the aircraft actually touched down, enabling accurate 'fixes' to be made for the rescue aircraft and vessels.

The first I heard of this disaster was from Reuters News Agency at my home in London (it had happened at the weekend). I arranged to charter a British aircraft to pick up the passengers and crew at Malta and to complete the journey to South Africa.

About two days after Lloyds had paid out the claim for the Dakota loss in full (£25,000), Creed placed the company under judicial management due to internal dissension, and thereafter it was only a matter of time before the company failed.

Early in 1952, before this happened, I had conceived the idea of forming a British company, and buying a war-surplus Dakota from the RAF at Silloth. The first shareholders were myself and my wife, Flo. I offered shares to Tom Meredith and Harry Creed. Creed declined, but Tom accepted. I also offered shares to Wally Thornhill, of Air Excursions and Charters, as well as German South Africa Airlines (in association with General von Mellenthin).

I had difficulty in having a name accepted by the Companies Registration Office. Eventually, at the suggestion of my solicitor, I submitted various combinations using the names of the three main shareholders: Hamilton, Meredith and Thornhill. As there was already a Hamilton Air Services and a Thornhill Aviation Transport Ltd in existence, I finally settled on Meredith Air Transport Ltd. This subsequently changed to African Air Safaris Ltd, as a more appropriate title.

I borrowed the money to start the company, and to buy the aircraft, from sources in the UK, under personal guarantee. I also brought in Davies and Newman Ltd (as I rented an office from them in the city). Captain Cas de Bounevialle (who flew the Avro York aircraft for Tropic on occasions) also joined as a minor shareholder. Captain de Bounevialle piloted the aircraft at all times and also acted as operations manager. I ran the company with the aid of one girl as an assistant, a Miss Joan Chapman. The company was also successful carrying out flights to South Africa and Rhodesia, as well as to other parts of the world. On Christmas Day 1952, when I was sitting down to Christmas lunch at my mother's home in Dumfries, I received a cable from Mike Keegan (an ex-BKS and now owner of Trans Meridian Air Cargo and British Air Ferries), saying that the aircraft had crashed at Jerusalem Airport whilst on a tour of the Middle East. Fortunately, it proved to be a minor accident, as Cas had found the only hole in the airfield with his tail-wheel.

Davies and Newman became seriously interested in aviation. They subsequently bought out Wally Thornhill's shares in the company. During the spring and summer of 1953, I received several letters from Tom Meredith, who was still in Johannesburg, asking me if I would like to join (and put money into) a new company about to be formed, as a shareholder and as a director (for Europe). At first I was not very keen, but eventually I agreed. This company was Trek Airways.

At this time, the Dakota was engaged in a lucrative and regular contract operating into Berlin, so I sold the aircraft and contract to Davies and Newman, who formed a separate company – Danair Services. I stayed as manager until just before Trek started operations. Danair is now one of the largest UK operators. The capital (£3,000) for my shares, Tom's shares and Cas de Bounevialle's shares in Trek came from the proceeds of this sale, and £1,000 was remitted to the Trek account in South Africa on 30 September 1953. A further £1,400 was remitted on 11 November to either Tom Meredith or Air Traffic (Pty) Ltd. The balance of £600 was used to set up and furnish a London office at 29 Whitehall (over the Silver Cross pub, near Trafalgar Square), to cover the initial expenses of operating this office.

On Christmas Eve 1953 I waited at Southend Airport all day for the arrival of the first Trek Dakota flight. On board as a passenger was another of the shareholders, whom I had not met, Fanie Botha (unfortunately now deceased). As I recall, the original shareholders were Paddy Rorke and Syd Excel (both of Phoenix Airways), Rod Rooken-Smith, Cecil Snelgar, Fred Gratz, Fanie Botha, Tom Meredith, Cas de Bounevialle and myself. At a later stage, Helm von Mellenthin was offered a shareholding. It was fairly soon that we bought out (or got rid of) Excel and Rooken-Smith. Fanie Botha got rid of us by selling our only Dakota over our heads during the summer of 1954, because of his personal financial problems.

This left us in a very difficult position, because we were heavily booked for months ahead. However, I was fortunate enough to charter several flights from Danair, pending the purchase of our first Viking 1A for about £11,000 from Airworks.

I arranged the finance through Lombard Bank over three years on my personal guarantee. (I was the only person resident in the UK on whom they could get their clutches in the event of default.)

Two further Vikings were purchased fairly rapidly thereafter, also through Lombard Bank, using African Air Safaris Ltd for all three. These three aircraft operated very successfully for us – despite engine failures at remote places such as Wadi Haifa, propellers being severely damaged on take-off at Benghazi or fabric tearing off the wings in flight. All these mishaps usually occurred at weekends. In 1968 we purchased two DC-4 aircraft from North West Airlines, once again using Lombard Banking, African Air Safaris Ltd and my personal guarantee. This time the amount involved was rather larger than before – about £250,000 in all – which included spares as well.

During 1956, before the DC-4 purchase, a decision was taken which almost caused the failure of the company – to buy a cocooned Hermes aircraft from BOAC for £80,000 (via Lombard AAS Ltd and my personal guarantee again) and have it put into a serviceable condition by Britavia Ltd. This cost another £64,000, but before it was completed, we discovered that the NTC would not give us permission to register it in South Africa or to operate it as Trek, because it was considered to be too competitive to SAA. This is a moot point, as it was a very expensive aircraft to operate. It was debatable whether we could have made a profit with it in any event.

Fortunately I managed to persuade Britavia Ltd to lease the aircraft from us for three years on an incredible basis, which prevented them from returning it to us or cancelling the lease until a certain number of landings had been made. They eventually found a way around this by using the aircraft on training 'circuits and bumps' – but in the interim we recouped the major part of our expenditure. The unfortunate Mr Barnes, who negotiated and signed the agreement, was subsequently sacked by Britavia.

One event which I still remember well happened during one of my visits to Johannesburg. I went into the office rooms to find Tom, Cecil and Fred, and two or three others whom I didn't know, sitting around a table. It transpired that they were discussing the formation of a new company to import farm pumping machinery from France (Peugeot, I think it was). They asked me if I would like to join in at a cost of £4,000. I pointed out that I would be of little use to them in London, but they said that I was not to worry on that score. They would all look after the business. I eventually agreed, and paid for my shares. A couple of years passed. I was on my way through Jan Smuts Airport with my family on holiday to Cape Town, when Cecil rushed over to me and asked me to sign a guarantee form. At first I refused. He said that this would put me in a bad light with the other participants – even though I had nothing to do with the running of the company. Soon afterwards, I was told that I owed £110,000 as a guarantor. Apparently they had employed a crooked salesman, who had put through bogus sales of pumps etc., and received bonuses accordingly. Without checking up, the shareholders and directors in Johannesburg (including Tom) had enthusiastically ordered a lot more pumps that couldn't be sold but had to be paid for. I had to pay my £110,000 by borrowing from Trek, as the rest did. It was deducted from future dividends. The name of the other man involved was Ackerman, who was reputed to be a millionaire with a car franchise. I never received the slightest sign of regret from anyone.

In February or March 1968, my family and I were on board the first DC-4 delivery flight, skippered by Cecil Snelgar and with Captain Iain Laatz, when an emergency landing was made at Wadi Seidna, near Khartoum. The following day, as the engines were being started to taxi over to pick up the passengers, a Sudanese ran into the starboard inner propeller and had his arm and head chopped off. Cecil was eventually brought before a Khartoum court. The unfortunate Arab was apparently the sole support of about thirty relatives, according to his lawyer!

Although at one stage we had landing and traffic rights at, and were operating from, Amsterdam, Düsseldorf, Paris, Nice, Vienna, Zürich, Rome and Athens, I was always very concerned about the erosion of these landing rights. The writing was on the wall when the Dutch authorities refused us permission to continue using Amsterdam unless we agreed to raise our fares to about 15% below IATA (International Air Transport Association). This we refused to do. We then made Düsseldorf our main European terminal. I started investigating the position at Luxembourg. I made first contact there with a Mr Hamer, head of the government department handling aviation matters. His assistant was Mr Hengen. Mr Joseph E Gurley was then the managing director of Luxembourg Airlines on behalf of Seaboard and Western Airlines (Scottish Aviation also had an interest in Luxembourg Airlines at this stage).

Landing rights were freely granted, an office was opened at Luxembourg and certain flights were routed there, although the link facilities were very poor at that time. It also first occurred to me at about that time that we should register a company and aircraft in Luxembourg, and operate from there. An American company, Interocean, had already done this. The field was wide open. Subsequently, due to Interocean's dubious activities and the emergence of Luxair as an airline in its own right under the able management of a young man, Roger Sietzen, the Luxembourg authorities began to change their views. Among names that were contemplated were Safari Airlines of Luxembourg and Luxembourg Air Services. Fortunately this idea was never followed up. I often wonder what would have transpired had we taken this step at that time.

In April 1960 I commenced negotiations with Mr Jean Dupong, then a director of Luxembourg Airlines, and with Mr Hamer, in connection with the franchise agreement between Trek and Luxembourg Airlines, whereby Trek was granted certain very valuable rights between Luxembourg and Southern Africa. It took until 29 May 1961 before the agreement was completely negotiated and signed, by myself and Mr D'Huart and Mr Dupong. Roger Sietzen had intervened in the latter stages. Part of the understanding was that we should register a Viking or a DC-4 (or both) in Luxembourg. A DC-4 (the only one remaining after its companion was written off in the Egyptian desert in the summer of 1960, piloted by Captain Laatz) was subsequently registered there. The franchise agreement paved the way for the first bilateral 'agreement' between Luxembourg and South Africa shortly afterwards.

It is interesting to note from a letter that I wrote to Mr Gurley in October 1956 how the development of Luxair from 1961 onwards followed rather similar lines to those I proposed at that time.

While Tom and I were based at Accra in the Gold Coast (as it was then) we flew the General Officer Commanding to Nigeria and then on to Sokotu, in the north. The emir of Sokotu offered us horses to ride. Tom had ridden before, and persuaded me to accompany him. This was not a very good idea as I didn't know one end of a horse from the other. He mounted his horse, and I attempted to mount mine, having great difficulty with the stirrups and reins. Tom took off on his horse – mine followed. I had only one foot in a stirrup and my hands were gripping the large pommel. The horse took off into the forest. I frantically held on while it attempted to brush me off against the trees and brushwood. The horse eventually stopped at its home village, about two miles away. I refused the kind offer to let me ride back. Needless to say, I walked very stiffly back to camp. This was my one brief encounter with a horse, yet today my youngest daughter, Samantha, is a BHS fully qualified riding instructor.

In Accra, the chief constable of police was a white man called Babe Llearoyd. He asked for volunteers to assist with the arrest of some blacks who were suspected of smuggling gold to Cairo, with some RAF help. Knowing that Tom was an ex-policeman he asked Tom for his help. I agreed to muck in. The police spy was recruited as our room attendant. He arranged a meeting with the prospective sellers in a mud hut in the 'staff' quarters one evening. We drove there in a jeep. On arrival we entered this mud hut, which was lit only by candles. There were about eight blacks sitting on the floor. One of them held a bottle of what appeared to be gold – but could have been brass filings for all we knew. The supposed signal for police intervention was that I should go outside to the jeep for something to weigh the gold that we were going to buy. After a few minutes I did that, but someone had forgotten to place a scale in the jeep and there was no sign of any police. I started to panic a little. Tom had a service pistol, but all I had was a lead cosh covered in leather, which I had bought as a souvenir in Cairo. However, I went back into the hut. Eventually, all hell broke loose, and resulted in the blacks being violently arrested. The one that had been holding the bottle of gold dropped it in an attempt to get out of a small opening in one wall, supposed to be a window. The bottle smashed and the gold was scattered all over the ground. Later at the police station we met the ringleader – if looks could kill, I wouldn't be around to recount this story. I certainly had some unusual experiences.

Another memory comes to mind. In 1946, after I was posted to Kenley, and operating to the war-devastated continent, it was customary for some of the crews to carry coffee beans and/or cigarettes to Hamburg and Berlin. On the Berlin route from Gatow Airport, the route our jeep took had to go through the Russian sector. We were often stopped and searched by the Russians. It was nearly all good-humoured, however, and they finished up with some coffee and cigarettes as a gift. It sounds a bit like a spy story, but the shop where we exchanged them for goods (including Meissen figurines, etc.) was operated by a beautiful blonde of about thirty, and a club-footed man. This was strictly against the law, of course, but I had never heard of anyone being caught. I wasn't astute enough to realise I could have made a small fortune. Instead, I spent the occupation money we were allowed on having a good time.

During my flights into and out of Israel during 1949, there was another story. There was a captain (he was a South African Jew married to a Maltese Roman Catholic) who became acquainted with a 'sabre' fighter pilot with one eye – he wore a black patch over the other one. After a few drinks they decided to take our Dakota for an air test, and at the same time to teach the 'sabre' how to fly it. Most of the crew came along but spent their time at the rear where the liquor supplies were. I, however, suspecting that the skipper had already had enough, decided to stay in the cockpit. We flew over Tel Aviv, which was forbidden, then over the bay at about 2,000 feet, with the fighter pilot at the controls. The skipper was relaxed in the first officer's position. Suddenly both engines cut – the aircraft proceeded towards the sea rather rapidly. The skipper was in an alcoholic daze, and the fighter pilot hadn't a clue what was wrong. I deduced that the main fuel tanks were empty. Hastily, I switched the emergency supply on. This involved working the 'wobble' pump to get the fuel to the engines. I frantically did this for what seemed an eternity. Finally, when the aircraft was about 200 feet from the surface of the water, the two engines burst into life again. Everyone heaved a sigh of relief.

I would like to mention that Derek Lawer, my personal assistant, joined the company in London in July 1957, after doing national service in the RAF; he had also trained as a travel agent. To date he has loyally been with the company almost seventeen years. He shared with me many traumatic experiences in this unpredictable aviation business.

As of 1974 Captain Cas de Bounevialle, after working with several companies that failed, became operations manager for a company in Barbados named 'Air Calypso' if you please! I hope for his sake it doesn't go bust as well.

I believe Captain Creed is a crop duster somewhere in Africa. He is well suited to this.

In 1958 three new British companies were formed: Safari Travel Ltd, which eventually absorbed the dormant African Air Safaris Ltd and which embraced South African Skytours, a company started by Paddy Rorke's brother, Bryan. An endeavour was made to start 'Inclusive Tours' with this company, but unsuccessfully.

Then there was the Safari Club Ltd, which took over large premises in Northumberland Grand Building, and operated as a social club initially for the benefit of South African visitors and residents in London.

Finally, Air Safaris Ltd, which was hived off from African Air Safaris Ltd as an operating company in its own right. This company took over two Vikings and the one Hermes (the other Viking went to Protea Airways) and operated many 'link' flights for Trek to the North African coast. It eventually and very unfortunately failed in 1961 due to over-rapid expansion, undercapitalisation and severe lack of proper financial control. If only I had known Alaistair Mackie then. I was chairman, Alan Stocks was MD and Cas de Bounevialle was operations director. I had far too much on my plate from 1958 to 1961, undoubtedly, and tried to achieve too much at once.

William Buckland 'Paddy' Rorke

This is a pen picture of my life.

All of Gaul was divided into three parts by Julius Caesar. My life in its earliest stages was divided into three parts.

1. 'The Years Before', concerning life as it was in South Africa in the early years of the twentieth century, up to 1930, when I finished secondary school education.
2. 'The Years Between', which began with the Great Depression.
3. The War Years (1939–1945)

The Years Before

My father was Claude Oriel Rorke. But let me begin with my great-grandfather. He was Rory O'Rourke of County Cork in the Emerald Isle. The economic state of Ireland in the nineteenth century was not great. Rory was worried about his three sons, as all he could offer them were the three Ps – potatoes, pigs and peat! Where was their future? It was when England began to organise the 1820 settlers that he saw a glimmer of light for his beloved offspring. This is how the three O'Rourke brothers landed up in the Cape Colony in South Africa – never to return to dear old Ireland!

As his sons boarded the ferry to England, Rory said, 'Always remember your Irish heritage and uphold our good name – but perhaps it may be advisable to change the spelling of our name slightly,' as from what he had heard he had gathered that the country with Dutch people would accept the name of Rorke more readily. So the wise Rory suggested that his sons drop the first 'O' and the 'U' and the new clan of the Rorkes was born. On arrival in South Africa the three boys did as their father had suggested and changed their surname to Rorke. Two of the brothers wandered off in search of adventure in Zululand, and ended up establishing a small trading store on the banks of a drift. They were well accepted in the sparsely populated state to such an extent that in time their domain became known as 'Rorke's Drift'. Little did they realise that their 'Rorke's Drift' was to become the one and the same 'Rorke's Drift' that was the venue of one of the bloodiest battles in world history. That hordes of Zulus would decimate the handful of brave Englishmen sent out by Queen Victoria to defend one of England's outposts. That thousands of assegais (spears), shields and bloodied Zulus would litter the South African veld. That the English Queen would gladly bestow no fewer than eleven Victoria crosses earned in one battle – a record never reached in all military history! *Sic transit Gloria mundi*! Few ever lived to receive their award but their names are surely recorded in the register of the almighty.

Claude Oriel was the second son of Benjamin William. He had been born in Somerset East in the Cape, having been schooled at Gill College. In 1907 he became engaged to Kathleen Elizabeth Jeanette Rocher of Huguenot extraction. She lived with her family in the original capital of the old Boer republic, Potchefstroom. They later farmed at Donderhoek in the Rustenburg area. Claude and Kathleen were engaged for seven years, and finally married in 1914. They moved to Witbank, fifty miles east of Pretoria, where my father joined his younger brother Jim in the Transvaal and Delagoa Bay mine (T&B) as a clerk.

I was born on 22 February 1915. Shortly after, my father apparently joined up with Louis Botha and Jan Smuts in the war zone.

My mother decided to join Claude's sister, Ella Buckland (hence my second name), in the Cape so off we set for Camps Bay. It was there two years later on the beach that my mother greeted a man in uniform and said, 'Paddy, this is your father.' The Rorke family now reunited, my father decided to move back to the Transvaal to Pretoria. We rented a house in Van der Byl Street. That was where I spent my earliest years, most happily.

Those were the days when one could buy two comics, *Puck* and *Rainbow*, for two pence. This was my introduction to reading.

It was those comics, strangely enough, that encouraged my love of reading, which was the case throughout my life.

In those days the entrance fee to the bioscope (not the cinema) was six pence. My other forms of entertainment were playing with the neighbours' two sons. We played 'tok-tokkie' and snakey – simple games, but they gave us a lot of fun. My father also used to take me to the municipal swimming baths, which were within walking distance from our home.

About this time the census of Pretoria had revealed that there were about 75,000 inhabitants.

In 1921 my brother, Bryan, was born. In 1923 my father purchased our first car – a T-model Ford. There were only two foot pedals; when one was pressed in, this was low gear. When it was gradually released while the car was in motion, it became the top gear. The other pedal was the brake. There was no self-starter – one had to use a crank handle. One had to be very careful to wrap one's thumb around the handle, as it was liable to backfire and could break the thumb. There were no windows, only side screens made of a celluloid substance, which were stored behind the front seats. They were to be used only in the cold weather or if it rained. There was only one windscreen wiper, to be operated manually with one hand while the other hand was used to steer the car. The maximum speed was 30 mph. Of course, the 'tin Lizzie', as it was called, had no spare wheel – only a spare rim fitted with a tyre. One changed rims, not wheels! Those were the days when tyres were easily prone to punctures.

In the early 1920s, according to today's standards, we were regarded as living in primitive conditions. For instance, there was no hot water laid on – in order to have a hot bath, we used to boil water in a paraffin tin on the coal stove in the kitchen. The toilet was outside, just off the *stoep* (veranda). There was no heating in most of the houses, so we used to sit huddled around a paraffin stove, or else sit in the kitchen which was usually the warmest place in the house. In winter, on account of the coal stove, which burnt almost continually, my young legs used to become badly chapped from the cold, so my mother used to make a mixture of paraffin and candle grease to ease the skin. It was quite effective – we were apparently accustomed to the somewhat pungent odour.

At night my parents had hot-water bottles but I had to be content with a brick heated in the oven and covered with an old towel – quite effective for a short period! I wore lace-up boots and thick black socks – only sissies wore shoes. In the summer the thick socks produced a smell from our feet – 'toe jam', we called it. Dad insisted that I sprinkle boracic powder between my toes. It certainly helped, but I was not particularly interested in the whole affair. Chemist accounts were unheard of in our household.

Every Sunday morning at 9 a.m. I would toddle off to the Christian Science Sunday School, always neatly clad – no jeans or open-necked shirts. Life was primitive, but we knew no better. In the afternoons my mates, Pierre and Victor, and I would often wander down to the nearby Apies River, where we would wander upstream and down, running up and down its concrete container sides. It was also fun to play amongst the reeds in our bare feet, chasing crabs and looking for the odd fish! During a summer storm the river had quite a bit of water (though certainly not a raging torrent). I found it difficult to credit that Winston Churchill, after his dramatic escape from the Staats Model School, had to swim across the Apies to escape. Why did he not just paddle across? This was always the story that we were told here in South Africa. (If we really had a terrific storm the Apies would actually become a raging torrent and it had been known for people to be swept away by the current and drown – a car had once also been swept away.)

In 1899 the late Sir Winston Churchill was assigned by the *Morning Post* as a war correspondent in the Boer War in South Africa. He was captured by Louis Botha in Natal, near Durban. He was imprisoned with other captured British officers in the Staats Model School in Pretoria. This building was close to the Apies River on the corner of Van der Walt and Skinner streets. Like all prisoners of war, escape was always uppermost in men's minds. Plans were always being made. Guard duty here appeared rather lax and highly inadequate. It had been observed that the eastern side of the school was a potential escape route. After close study, a plan was made. It was noted that the Boers on patrol lost portions of the compound from their vision. Hence, Winston and two other officers decided to scale the eastern wall and head for the British line on Delagoa Bay, which was in Portuguese territory. This journey was estimated to be about 300 miles.

Churchill and fellow prisoners Captain Haldane and Lieutenant Brockie made their plans. Winston was the first over the wall, hid in the foliage nearby. When his companions did not follow, Winston decided to proceed on his own. He broke cover and openly walked along a street, completely unchallenged. He thought he was less likely to look like a fugitive if he behaved in that manner. This he did until he reached a small bridge across the Apies River with only £75 and some chocolate in his pocket. Winston, guided by the stars, proceeded in what he thought was a southerly direction.

Fortune smiled on him. Fairly soon, he stumbled upon a railway track, which he followed hoping that he was heading in the right direction. Eventually arriving at a small station, he decided to attempt to board the first train, hoping that this transport would take him closer to freedom. Eventually a train arrived, stopping at the station. As the train drew off again, Winston managed to mount one of the trucks. Favourably, he had struck a goods train containing empty coal bags – an ideal hiding place. Here Winston settled and was soon lulled into sleep by the motion of the train. It was still dark when he surfaced from his slumbers.

He decided his next plan would be to try and get some idea as to his whereabouts. Hoping for the best, he jumped from his truck. He landed unhurt. Dawn soon came in the eastern skies – *mirabile dictu*. The trains had been going in the right direction, towards the Portuguese border.

Another train was boarded. This time Winston hid under bales of wood. This uncomfortable journey he endured for another three days, finally arriving in Lourenco Magues, where the British were stationed. This journey had taken eleven days. Winston reported to the British consul, who made arrangements for Winston to go by sea to Durban, a sea port in Natal. Churchill was back, close to the place where he had originally been captured by the Boers. So much for the myth that Sir Winston Churchill swam the Apies River to freedom from the Staats Model School.

Sir Winston died in London, 24 January 1965. He received a state funeral, the first for a commoner since 1898.

I have digressed and so will continue with my own saga, about life in Pretoria in the early days.

The common form of transport in the absence of a railway was by a clanging tram. Taxis there were, but not as we know them today. A taxi was a horse-drawn hansom cab: what a joy it was if our parents sent us to fetch one from the marketplace – a free ride inside relaxing on the luxuriously padded seats while the cabby sat high up on his outside perch, reining his two precious horses. Pure delight!

On the roads, electric trams gave way to petrol-driven buses; robots (traffic lights to the outside world) were installed and speed limits were introduced. Progress! So the world went from one wonder to the next.

Indoor distractions were few. In rainy weather or after dark we would play games like snakes and ladders, tiddlywinks, ludo or snap. Our reading, when not Enid Blyton, would be the weekly English comics – *Puck* or *Rainbow*, with Tiger Tim and his jolly companions. In later years we read Jeffrey Farnol, Baroness Orczy or Edgar Wallace. At least our minds were being exercised. As our teens began my father taught us 'nap', a five-card game that served as an introduction later to bridge. To exercise our intellects, we and our mates often played charades.

Our weekly treat was the arrival of the mail from England, introducing us in the *Gem* to the schoolboy world of St Jim's with Tom Merry and his mates, or the *Magnet* depicting school life at Greyfriars with Bob Cherry and the inimitable, notorious and fatuous Billy Bunter. Alas, in the mid-twentieth century these publications ceased, and schoolboys were deprived of valuable lessons of sportsmanship, gamesmanship and fair play – to be replaced by today's endless and often mindless TV offerings of *skop, skiet en donder* (kick, shoot and violence). A strut has been taken away from the structure of adolescent schoolboys (and girls): instead, the fires of crime, deceit and selfishness have been fuelled. More's the pity!

1921 brought a bitter disappointment. In February I would be six and ready for school. This was a dream that I had cherished – I would at last be able to read and I would have fun at school away from home. But, alas, the education people raised the school age to six and a half years. I was devastated – I had to wait another whole year. No one had heard of preschool, kindergarten or baby schools.

But 1922 at last arrived and off to Sunnyside School I went. An ambitious headmaster decreed that the top student at the end of six months should not be held back to sit around with the rest of the class but should move to the next grade. That is how in December 1925 I finished with the primary school. On I moved to Pretoria Boys High School and in 1930 waved a matriculation certificate. My years of secondary schooling, with their cricket, rugby and athletics, were over. With a breaking heart I said farewell to my mates of years and prepared for a university career.

The Years Between

As the third decade of the century dawned, few in the world could suspect what lay before them in the next fateful ten years. Except possibly in the United States where the Wall Street crash of 1929 was already to take its toll.

For me the sun shone brightly on New Year's day of 1931. God was in His heaven – and I would shortly be in Grahamstown – a town of history, of culture, with schools of renown throughout our land and of religion, with at least forty churches and chapels. Although my old headmaster had strongly advised that I should wait a year before going to university, on account of my age, I had my way. I concealed my tender years, joined wholeheartedly in university life, and for the first six months was happy – contented and carefree, but never beyond the pace of seemly and acceptable behaviour! I studied my commerce and accounting, and even found time to relax in the university library with the historical works of William Shakespeare. Polonius would always remind me of Billy Bunter, whom I had enjoyed reading about in the days when I had read *Gem* and *Magnet* – comics which, as mentioned, are alas today denied our youths in favour of so many mindless television shows with sex and violence.

But my euphoria was rudely interrupted when in the July

vacation at home my father explained the pall of the Depression, which even South Africa had now inherited from the American catastrophe. The Goldfields Building Society, whose branch he managed, was insolvent, its chairman resorting to suicide. My dad was without a job or income. It was then that I began to realise the gravity and misery of almost everyone's situation. As my annual dues had already been settled with Rhodes, I was permitted to return for the final miserable semester. I passed all my subjects and returned with a heavy heart to take up articles with a worldwide firm of chartered accountants, Price Waterhouse and Peat.

So the decade of the years between was launched in misery and despair. Slowly, very slowly did the pall lift, and open the way to the joyful days of the mid-thirties, with wondrous new advances in science, in medicine and indeed in all fields of human endeavour. Music was tuneful, peace was now everywhere, business was booming and everyone had a smile on their lips. Happy days were here again! I was also happy, but oh so busy – serving articles for six days each week, attending extramural classes at Pretoria University until 10 p.m., but still at the weekends keeping up my cricket, rugby and even baseball.

1936 saw me as a qualified chartered accountant, with a B.Com degree and even becoming an associate of the Chartered Institute of Secretaries. It was the year when I turned twenty-one that my old dad arranged a celebratory dance in my honour, a jolly occasion, in which I met my future wife – and also the year in which my father passed away from a heart attack. More than that, it was the year in which my articles were completed and I was forced to look for a new means of earning a livelihood.

Yet one other event occurred which was to affect me throughout the whole of my career. An old school pal of mine, Brian Gibson, was also aspiring to become a CA, serving articles in a small practice. As often as possible we would lunch together. He had become interested in the stock exchange and explained to me the import of an 'Ex London' transaction. Before the days of airmail and telex, if a South African dealt on the London Stock Exchange he would only be called to settle his investments after a lapse of thirty days – wonderful gambling for bulls and bears! I was fascinated, especially when Brian invited me to join him in speculating with a tip which he had received.

We jointly bought 400 Reef Nigel Gold shares at five shillings and sixpence (5s 6d), held them nervously for ten days, sold at eight shillings and pocketed the money – money for jam! I was hooked, and ever after studied the stock exchange ticker. I bought and sold Ex London, even before I came of age. As a matter of fact, the first cheque that I ever drew when I became eligible to open a bank account was to my brokers, Wyllie and Mortimer.

By the end of 1936 I knew that I was a financial fundi – I had made some thousands of pounds. It was easy and I was a capitalist! But I had completely forgotten my father's explanation of the New York crash of 1929.

I thought it could not happen here – but it did! For long before the Christmas of 1936 I proudly held 4,000 Western Reef Gold Mine shares. They showed me a fair profit at the current price of ninety-six shillings. Rumours emanating from America about gold disconcerted me, and I decided to realise my profits. Next afternoon at 3.30 p.m., I nervously suggested to the young lady behind the counter at Wyllie and Mortimer that I should place a selling order, as my shares had dropped back to ninety shillings. 'Paddy,' she said, 'why not see what happens tomorrow morning? It is nearly closing time.' I waited – she frantically phoned me early next morning. 'Paddy, you had better come round quickly.' Western Reefs had opened at sixty shillings. All my profits from the past had gone, and I owed my brokers £1,000 – I did not even have 1,000 pennies! Luckily I persuaded them to allow me to liquidate my debts at £25 per month. For three whole years I had this albatross round my neck. The ignorance and folly of youth!

1937 dawned bleakly for me. I was jobless, my father had died, leaving an estate of only £400, and no residence after the big depression, I had a young brother still in school, and I was now the sole breadwinner – not to mention my albatross! Men in such circumstances have been known to commit suicide. But I was too full of self-confidence even to contemplate such a thought – somehow I would win through.

As the New Year started I squared my shoulders and heard that Mr McGillivray, a small-time practising CA, was looking for a partner. He accepted me at a salary of thirty pounds per month plus a quarter share of the profits (if any) – but I was to pay a premium of £500 for goodwill, to be liquidated out of my share of profits. I at least had a job, and even the prospect of one day inheriting the practice from the ageing Mr McGillivray. I was almost solvent – but what about income for the family?

I had been in the practice for ten days, while the deed of partnership was being drawn up by an attorney. If this had been some twenty years later, I would have drawn up my own partnership deed – I have scant faith in the legal fraternity when it comes to financial matters.

Brian Gibson came as usual to go out to lunch, and before leaving we repaired to the toilet. As we stood and did our business Brian asked if I had already signed the partnership agreement. 'Be careful,' he said, 'don't let the old bugger tie you up too closely – remember we want to be in partnership together one day.' I nodded.

I was called to Mr McGillivray's office on my return. He had overheard Brian's remark in the loo. I was out on my ear! The tight-fisted Scot never even paid me one penny for my ten days' work. In those days I was too naive to demand my rights.

Out on the street, again jobless, I went home to tell my poor mother about the disaster. She, strange to relate, was helpful, and referred me to a fellow church member of hers who owned a large department store and was looking for a capable accountant. Mr George Murray was a senior partner in Beckett Murray, a well-respected store in Church Street in the centre of Pretoria. I was given a month's trial to see if I, at the tender age of twenty-two, could cope with a large office and eight female clerks – Mr Murray was doubtful. I could cope, and so I started at twenty-seven pounds ten shillings per month, hardly a fortune for a qualified CA. But George Murray was a canny Scot (as Mr McGillivray had also been). I was in no position to bargain! I spent eighteen happy months at Beckett Murray, learning a lot about merchandising in a departmental store and had good practice at originating accounting entries instead of merely auditing what appeared in someone else's books. It was good experience for me!

My income was not sufficient to keep the family and me afloat; I had to supplement it. Not only did I have to service my albatross, but my father on his deathbed had told me of an obligation with which he had been landed when his Goldfields Building Society folded. An aged cousin of his, Aunt Emily, had invested her life savings in the building society and was left penniless. Although this was not Dad's fault, he nevertheless felt obliged to promise to give her a monthly pension of fifteen pounds. He looked to me to fulfil his promise – little did he know of my precarious financial situation. I had to agree before he closed his eyes and passed away. Another albatross!

Pretoria has always been an Afrikaans-orientated city, and now as rumours of war filled the air and racism abounded, its Pretoria University felt behoved to switch from bilingual tuition and become a totally Afrikaans-speaking institution. The professor of accounting was solely English speaking, and had to be replaced. They advertised the post and wanted the appointee not only to lecture in Afrikaans but also to be in public practice as a CA and furthermore to have an academic degree. Even my old boss had been somewhat scathing about my attending extramural classes – 'After all, a CA has far more prestige than a university degree,' was his dictum. Luckily I had ignored him, and was now the only practising CA in Pretoria who could fulfil all the university's demands. I appeared before the senate presided over by a Dr Arndt, who had recently published the first Afrikaans Commercial Dictionary. When the good doctor asked how I would cope with all the commercial terms in my lectures, I replied, 'By using your dictionary, of course – and what is more I shall insist on each student buying your book.' The number of students in my class would approximate 200. Dr Arndt's financial mouth must have watered at my proposal. I got the job – but only at eight pounds, six shillings and eight pence per month. Times were still hard.

I subsequently landed a lectureship at Pretoria Technical College and in addition wrote a correspondence course for a private institution called University Correspondence College. For rewriting their accounting lectures I was paid an hourly rate. In addition, at the end of each lecture, I set questions to be answered. For marking these, I received a handsome sixpence per question. I set five questions at the end of each lecture, which earned me 2s 6d per paper – there were many papers to be marked. Naturally I made sure that at least two questions could be marked by a cursory inspection of less than a minute.

By the end of 1937 I was a very busy 22-year-old – I repaid my stockbroker in two years, and for Aunt Emily I arranged a pension. At least our family could eat, and my brother could finish his schooling before the war arrived in 1939. It was indeed a sweat, but still I managed. During the weekends I contrived to play my cricket, hockey and baseball. The dignity of work! My greatest sorrow during the decade was that I was unable to afford either money or time to marry the light of my life, Ticatic Dreyer. She had an unusual name, but then she was an unusual girl, and I was deeply in love! Sadly she had an impetuous streak and when she matriculated from Pretoria Girls High (she had been Head Girl), she had a disastrous row with her callous father, ran away from home and suddenly married an older man who was a newspaper editor. I know, and she told me, that she would far rather have married me, but I was in no way yet eligible and she was desperate. It broke my heart as she moved to the distant Orange Free State. For seven long years she disappeared from my ken.

I did indeed many months later meet a delightful younger girl from a German family of immigrants, Hilda Wolff. The rebound, no doubt! I learned to appreciate the Germans, spent many happy days in their delightful home, and was regarded by her father as an acceptable prospective son-in-law. The old man, as the war clouds gathered in Europe, would on Sunday nights buttonhole me in front of his radio to listen to Hitler's broadcasts from Zeesen. In between the deafening applause from the crowds, Mr Wolff would interpret the Führer's words. He almost persuaded me to believe in the Nazis, but never quite! I loved Hilda in a brotherly sort of way, but had no thought of marriage. She understood that my heart belonged to Ticatic, however much in vain this might seem. It was not many years later that Hilda was also lost to me – she passed away suddenly from a brain tumour. I was devastated.

Before the end of my adventurous decade I was to experience

yet another transformation. Grateful as I was to Beckett Murray for giving me sustenance, I was not altogether content with my sphere of work. The job could well have been done by a competent bookkeeper, after I had installed an efficient system of accounting records. This is possibly why George Murray had seen fit to advance my remuneration to only thirty-two pounds ten shillings per month, even though he often expressed satisfaction with the myriad figures which he constantly sought from me. Although I would hesitate to call my principal tight-fisted, a canny and careful Scot he undoubtedly was! He did indeed suggest that in time to come I might well acquire an interest in his flourishing concern. To me this was too indefinite and too far-seeing to satisfy my self-imposed ambition. After all, I was a CA. Although at present far removed from auditing, I felt that urge to return to the profession, now my twin albatrosses had been dealt with.

An opportunity presented itself. One of Pretoria's highly respected and financially rewarded surgeons was in need of an accountant and income tax consultant. He offered me the part-time appointment for a monthly fee of thirteen guineas. It sorely tempted me, but while employed by Beckett Murray I could not accept. I cut the Gordian knot, resigned, rented an office for fifteen pounds per month and publicly announced that I was once again in practice. Proudly I painted 'W B Rorke and Company' on the street window of my downstairs office facing Bank Lane. It was a hazardous step, but boldness be my friend! The company part of my firm consisted of Audrey Pieterson, my costing clerk who begged me to take her with me. She was a gem and for many years expertly typed my financial statements. To my surprise George Murray was cooperative, and agreed to pay me a retainer to initiate his son, Ian, into my job. Grist to the mill!

Brian Gibson in the meantime was still always in touch, contrite for his part in terminating my partnership with Mr McGillivray. In the interim he too had qualified, and was now a junior partner of his erstwhile boss, Mr Paxton – another canny Scot! Their practice consisted mostly of military audits. They were the official auditors of all messes and canteens within the orbit of Pretoria Military Headquarters. As the war was looming closer and closer, more and more military camps were being established, creating a host of messes and canteens. Paxton and Gibson were battling to keep pace with the expansion. My branching out on my own was a heaven-sent relief to them. We agreed that I assist them two days a week for a split of the fees. In addition I had managed to find three other clients to audit. I never had a dull moment – W B Rorke and Co. was on its way!

On the fateful Sunday of 3 September 1939, I had just hurried home from the Wolffs to listen to Neville Chamberlain's ominous announcement. It was war! No longer 'peace in our time' as Hitler had prompted the gullible English prime minister to exclaim, as he waved his umbrella from his aircraft returning from Germany. How Hitler hoodwinked him!

The die was cast and the years between were now at an end.

The War Years

The six years from 1939 brought war and tears into so many lives, and into my life they brought endless toil, blood and sweat. Those days after the tragic death of Hilda, my association with her family (in itself a sadness) came to an end – my freedom from financial anxiety also improved and there was a happy ending as Ticatic again came back into my life.

In cooperation with Brian Paxton and Gibson my professional career began to take shape. It was in 1940 that a far-reaching transition occurred.

One evening Brian and I had returned to the office from interviews at Defence Headquarters with Brigadier Ross, in charge of all messes and canteens under the Pretoria command. He had us to procure for him two members of our profession, to be appointed as supervisors of his military summoned establishments, each with the rank of captain. The matter was on our minds as we tuned into the news service on the office radio. A flash report was suddenly announced. Mussolini had joined Hitler – Italy was in the war! 'Bloody hell!' exclaimed Brian. 'The fat is now in the fire!' The cold war was now ended – the battle would be long and hard. It did not take us long to resolve that now was the hour to forget about our practices, and join in the enlistment rush that was bound to follow. How better than with captain pips under Brigadier Ross! In the morning we rushed to

HQ only to find that the colonel had overnight appointed one captain for Brigadier Ross. There remained only one opening, and the rank had been reduced to that of lieutenant, two pips. We tossed a coin, Brian won, and left a note on Mr Paxton's desk. 'I have joined up! Goodbye.' The Brigadier assured us that soon another vacancy would occur. I agreed to wait.

It was on the following day that two things happened. Brian telephoned to say that Mr Paxton had kicked him out of the partnership – unpatriotic and a completely illegal act in wartime. Another Scotsman, thought I! But Brian was laconic. 'None of us might survive – so what the hell!' The second happening was an urgent call for me to come to Mr Paxton's office. He had the effrontery to offer me the partnership which he had yesterday terminated with Brian. I was livid! Discussion brought solution – I would accept his offer, provided he reinstated Brian as a third partner. It was agreed with one proviso, and one which scotched my hopes of an army career. I must agree not to enlist – which is how I lost my dream of a VC, and was chained to my desk for the duration of the war.

The new partnership proved to be an unholy alliance. Mr Paxton had only vague views of accountancy, having been admitted to the Society of Accountants in 1905, when its founding bill offered membership to all practising bookkeepers, irrespective of their accounting ability or knowledge. Some months later, the ageing Mr Paxton withdrew from our partnership to take up a position offered to him by St Andrew's Building Society.

Brian and I were now at last in partnership, as we had envisaged that fateful day in the loo. In the interim Brian had managed to wangle a transfer to the air force and, with his wings, was already flying in Ethiopia, unaware of his new status. I wrote to Addis Ababa, telling him of the new firm of Gibson and Rorke, in which we shared profits equally, provided that he would pay in his military salary. I felt I owed it to Brian to put his name first in our title. By 1945, Gibson and Rorke was a household name in all messes and canteens in Pretoria and as far afield as Sonderwater and beyond. Many a night did I, with my four or five clerks, sleep in military barracks. We became inured to the jibes of those in uniforms who secretly envied our freedom, oblivious of our hard daily slogging over figures. Often would we be summoned to give evidence in court martial, where some errant caterer was charged with confusing his private foods with those of the army.

Recruitment of office staff to assist in the audits was a constant headache. All the best had long since enlisted, and I was left to salvage the dregs; clerks who not only could cope with the books but also who were loyal to the government's war effort. Many there were who would seek to sabotage if granted access to military establishments, so I had to choose with care! Nevertheless Gibson and Rorke, like Alice in Wonderland, grew and grew, as even commercial audits kept rolling in – office hours in daylight expanded into overtime at night-time. It was not easy! Far rather would I have been winging through the clouds over the far-flung states or Africa, as Brian was doing – not in battle, but merely in transport, leaving much time for friendly relaxation in cosy officers' messes, glass in hand. Lucky Brian – I should have called tails. But I survived and even prospered.

As I at last discarded my Wyllie and Mortimer albatross, and as Aunt Emily had quietly passed on to pastures new, I began to feel the jingle of coins in my pockets, could repay my bank and once again breathed fresh air. My mother, sensing the easing of tension, begged me to assist an old friend of hers. Lottie Faure had been deserted by her husband and had been saddled with three daughters to educate. This she had for years now done by opening a quiet hairdressing salon in Hatfield. She could not afford assistants and had to struggle with antiquated equipment which was scarcely adequate. Lottie was no longer young, and she was tired – weary not only from the strain of work, but more so from the ever-present fear that her meagre takings might not equate to her monthly commitments. I advanced her funds to refurnish her premises in a modest way. More importantly, I guaranteed her a monthly salary. She was grateful, and I felt virtuous, not so much caring whether my half-share of profits (if any) would cover even the interest on my outlay.

Our partnership outlived the war, until in 1945 she announced her daughters were now off her hands, and asked if I would buy her out by giving her a small pension. I could hardly refuse. I had in all innocence acquired a new albatross! In matters of the salon's takings, financial statements and tax returns, I was well schooled. About cutting, shampooing and permanent waving of the locks, I was not only abysmally ignorant but also completely uninterested. However, an advertisement in the Johannesburg *Star* introduced me to Paul Trisk, a recent immigrant from Golders Green in London, a man in search of employment and, mirabile dictu, a hairdresser!

I floated 'Salon de Paul (Pty) Ltd', provided Paul and his wife with a motor car and a rented house, advanced the company enough to renovate the salon's premises to Paul's somewhat extravagant satisfaction, and sat back to await results. We agreed to share profits equally, and I granted my new partner a reasonable salary. I was not disappointed. Paul soon emerged as a magnet to all socially climbing housewives, seeking tonsorial splendour. No ambitious women in the posh eastern suburbs could be without his artistic touches. Our takings soared. Where Lottie had been grateful to earn five pounds on a good day, Paul grumbled if he netted less than thirty pounds per day, and would collect and bank his cash. He emphatically turned down my suggestion of a cash register. Each evening I made out a cash slip for every customer, and put a duplicate in my daily cash. A cash register was a pure waste of money. I should have known otherwise, but was still naive and unsuspecting, unschooled in the cut and thrust of the tough world of business.

For two years our profits escalated, and Christmas brought a handsome dividend. So successful had we been in two years, that Paul had shown his ambitious nature by opening a second salon in the neighbouring suburb of Brooklyn. Its name, 'Razzelles', was that of his wife. I was pleased that my immigrant associates had so soon become satisfied with our South African way of life and business. By this time my investment in the hairdressing trade had become quite substantial. I was due a considerable sum by the two companies by way of my loan account for advances made by me for capital expenditure.

At the beginning of 1947 Paul Trisk dropped his bombshell. He was not satisfied with two suburban salons – he wanted to start in the centre of Pretoria, and he no longer needed my financing. He demanded that I buy out his half-share in both companies. The price he demanded was an impossibly high figure for his share of the goodwill. I was flabbergasted at his perfidy and lack of gratitude for all that I had done to put him on his feet. Shakespeare was right: 'Blow, blow, thou winter wind, / Thou art not so unkind / As man's ingratitude.'

I was in a stick as cleft as that of the foremost native runners. Who could I ever find to run both businesses to ensure repayment of my considerable loan account?

Then providence intervened in the form of Jessie Froneman, our senior assistant in the business, and whose husband was a client of my practice. Hearing of Paul's demands, Jessie told me in confidence that for many months Paul had been pocketing a portion of each day's takings. His most lucrative income was from perms for women who adored his work and never dared question his charges. Where Lottie had permed for a modest three guineas, Paul had a fluctuating scale adjusted to suit each individual client. Never less than eight guineas, but should an unfortunate madam arrive in a Mercedes it would be hiked to ten guineas. It would be beneath her to query his charge. 'She could well afford it,' was Paul's dictum.

Jessie stated that Paul on average performed not less than eight perms each day, of which two or three went into his own pocket. He then destroyed the slips. 'Two for you and one for me' no doubt was his motto.

With my new wife, we devised a plan. She offered eight of her friends free perms at Salon de Paul. They would have to pay but would be reimbursed afterwards. The only provision was that they must be prepared to sign affidavits regarding their payments, and further, they must be prepared to testify in court if necessary.

On the selected day all eight ladies attended. I collected the takings as usual at closing time. In the car with me I had a detective from the police CID. I parked in such a way that he had a clear view of the handing over of the cash. In the car we opened the cash bag and found only five slips for perms. Paul had stolen three perms from the company, worth thirty guineas. The detective immediately arrested him in the salon.

As Paul cringed in fear, the detective muttered in Afrikaans,

'*Hierdie man is 'n Jood!*' (This man is a Jew.) To me this came as a great surprise. I am in no way anti-Semitic, but I have frequently in the past been warned to be ultra-cautious in dealing with Jewish or Scottish businessmen. I am not canny enough to cope with their shrewdness. One lives and learns!

Paul actually cried to me in terror lest he be gaoled or, worse still, be deported back to England, from this land of milk and honey. I made a bargain with him. He could retain the Salon de Paul provided he paid me out the same sum which he had demanded from me. Fair is fair! Razzelles! I would take over completely in lieu of all the money which he had stolen over the years. He had no option but to pay me out. Razzelles I donated to Jessie Froneman for her valuable assistance. For years she ran it for her own account. She was ecstatic! The only hurdle which I had to surmount was in keeping Paul out of court. One may not compound a crime. Luckily I had an attorney-general friend from whom I had bought Tileba Township. He managed to squash the case, although how, I never found out.

I had washed my hands successfully of the hairdressing trade. I was unscathed and not out of pocket. Paul soon after sold Salon de Paul. I heard that he had opened in the centre of Johannesburg, but never again did I ever hear anything from him or about him. To this day I often wonder how he finally landed up. No skin off my nose! I did not grieve his absence.

My first experience outside the world of accountancy was now complete. Little did I realise that during the war period I would have other adventures into the field of business, culminating in Trek Airways. But much water was still to flow under my bridge.

To say this was my first extra-accountancy experience is not entirely correct. While I was still employed at Beckett Murray I never lost my interest in the stock exchange. With the albatross of Wyllie and Mortimer stiff round my neck, I nevertheless visited their offices almost daily to keep up with ticker trends. With the mounting fears of a coming conflict, business on the bourse was dead; in comparison the dodo was a lively bird! One afternoon the girl behind the counter at the brokers told me sadly that they had not had a single client the whole day. To placate her I took a ten-pound note from my pocket, and placed an order to buy as many

B Far East Gold shares as the note would cover. Their price was one penny – how much further could they drop!

Back in the office I told my secretary jokingly what I had done. It came as a tremendous surprise when, some days later, I learned that all the office staff, as well as some of the sales staff, had rushed in to buy B Far East. 'Mr Rorke knows the stock exchange – he must have some inside information,' was apparently the general whisper. What could I say? I just pitied them for their blind confidence in my financial acumen. It was many months later that for some unexplained reason the shares went up to thirty-two pence. We all sold, and I was dubbed a financial fundi. Life is sometimes like that!

In the early days of W B Rorke and Company I had acquired the Pretoria agency of London Assurance. It was always useful for a practising accountant to have a sideline in insurance. Many of his clients leave their insurance cover in the hands of their auditor.

The local agent of London Assurance had offered me his unimpressive insurance portfolio for the sum of £400. I had no money, but nevertheless phoned the head office in Johannesburg. This is how I met Roisen John Sater, who drove from Johannesburg just to meet me. I found Roy to be not only a shrewd businessman and a canny Scot, but also of a likeable disposition and a pleasure to talk to. He laughed at his Pretoria agent's price of £400. 'That man's a complete flop – we have sacked him.' I was surprised to hear Roy transferred his Pretoria agency to me for free. For many years I was able to influence a moderate amount of business to London. But ours was a personal connection which lasted through many years, resulting in not a few business dealings in partnership.

My second sally into the world of economic activity came in 1940. In my frequent visits to keep pace with the stock market, I had cultivated many ticker acquaintances. One was Mr McDowell, another canny Scot, a cautious businessman, and the owner of a flourishing stationery firm called Allardice and Harley. He was evidently well heeled, and he used to talk proudly of a valuable business stand which he owned in the centre of Pretoria, opposite the local magistrate's court. He had held it for many years at a cost of £11,000, but was convinced that in time it would be worth more than double. In fact he was disturbed at the war news, and was looking for a buyer at £25,000. I used to pull his leg by offering him £18,000 – I could not at that time scratch up 18,000 pennies. It was my idea of a bit of fun with a money-grabbing Scotsman.

On the day before the 1940 budget speech by the Minister of Finance, Jannie Hofmeyer, he asked me what I knew about the proposed new war tax on the sale of fixed property. With tongue in cheek, I said glibly, 'Anyone selling fixed property after tomorrow will have to pay all profit to the government.' I saw McDowell blanch, but was surprised to hear him say, 'Are you still interested in my ground at £18,000?' I nodded, more to repeat my leg-pull than in earnestness. As he rushed out he said over his shoulder, 'I'll phone you this afternoon.' I could not believe it!

Back in my office I urgently phoned Roy Sater. When I explained matters, Roy said that I must go ahead and make an offer – he would arrange finance – we would go into the deal fifty-fifty. Next morning, two hours before the budget speech, I signed a deed of sale. We had indeed made a real bargain. Sure enough the budget did introduce a fixed property profit tax, but it only applied to land purchased after the date. Mr McDowell was furious. 'Paddy, you bastard – you have conned me!' My reply was simply, 'How could I read the minister's mind?' Nuff said. He was extremely annoyed with me.

On the stand were three battered shops. I would each month collect the meagre rentals, and Roy and I would jointly make up the difference to meet our building society bond instalment. This went on year after year until 1949 – long after the armistice, the government made us an offer of £37,000. We were not satisfied, as our asking price was £45,000.

Then came the 1949 general election. General Smuts was beaten at the polls, in much the same way as the English Winston Churchill. The United Party government fell; the Nationalists took over the reins of government. I panicked – perhaps the new party in control would no longer be interested in our ground. Post-haste I raced up to the Union buildings and signed for £37,000. A drop in price certainly, but a handsome profit for Roy and myself. It was the first of our joint deals – more were to follow.

As the war in Europe escalated into the bombing of Britain, military command in South Africa in 1940 initiated the National Volunteer Brigade. All loyal supporters of the war effort who could not be spared to enlist full-time joined the NVB. We would parade one evening a week, have shooting practice and attend weekend camps. Once having been taught the elements of warfare we would be deputed to guard important government installations each night. Every week I and my cronies, all lowly privates, would take on two-hour shifts of sentry duty at the Union buildings, power station and other points of importance. The anti-war element in the country was vociferous and subversively active. Through the war we followed this programme as an extra duty over and above our daily occupations. Incidentally the captain in charge of our detachment was Captain McDowell, the very same – he never mentioned a word about our property deal to me. I am sure he was still inwardly sore with me, but he was man enough to push it far back in his mind. For this I admired him, dour and canny Scot though he was!

It was one night when I was on guard duty in darkness and solitude at the back of the Union buildings that I defied regulation and at 3 a.m. stopped to speak to the fellow recruit on the adjoining beat. Bill Vanlet was an immigrant from Holland. The Netherlands had decreed that Dutch nationals in any country should be commandeered for duty in the Dutch East Indies. Japan was now in the fray. Bill was leaving next week. He had philosophically accepted his country's call-up, but was grieved that he still had fifty stands to sell in Valhalla, for which he was employed as the sole selling agent. He told me that the average selling price was £125 per stand. What his principal would do after his departure, Bill did not know. His was a specialised job and, with the war on, it would be virtually impossible for his boss to replace him. Sales would stagnate. I asked whether he thought the owner would accept a package deal at seventy-five pounds per stand. Bill replied, 'He'll probably have no option – yes!' Soon after Brian's enlistment I had managed to acquire the Pretoria agency for the Provincial Building Society – a Natal concern. I had been asked to form a local board of three prominent Pretoria businessmen. This I had done. For inclusion in the new board I had nominated William Macintosh, a most successful local hardware merchant. Another canny Scot, he was reputed to be a millionaire!

Coming off duty from the NVB that night with Bill Vanlet, I next floated Pretoria Enterprises (Pty) Ltd in company with Roy Sater and Bill Macintosh. My third share in the company I decided to share with Brian. The other two between them provided all the finance. After all this I felt it was only fair to cut Brian in, serving as he was somewhere in North Africa, with no opportunity to make deals. Pretoria Enterprises (Pty) Ltd was no pushover. Within a month sinkholes began to appear in Valhalla, a suburb south of Pretoria. Overnight one whole house dropped twenty feet into a gaping hole. How was I to know that the whole of Valhalla was undermined by dolomite, with large caves under the entire property?

It took us years to dispose of our stands and to coax buyers back with the assurance that the worst was over and the houses would be safe. The war was over by the time that we sold our last stand. We recovered our investment; but from my point of view it was an exercise in futility. I had all the headaches, and the profit was minimal. This was my second venture with Roy.

The third exploit with Roy came not long after we had realised our profit from the sale of McDowell's property. We each had received 8,000 from the deal – not inconsiderable in those early post-war years before galloping inflation.

I was adamant that my new-found fortune would not be squandered on the stock exchange. I would invest in fixed property – terra firma – and the firmer it was, the less terror there would be! Roy wanted me to join him in a share deal. I refused. Naturally he made a quick profit while my money languished in the bank. Ah well, life is like that!

Eventually I was offered a tract of land in Pretoria North, owned by the local attorney-general. The price was fair, it had been passed as a township. All we had to do was to develop and sell. Easy meat! But it turned out to be another headache, a pup that I had bought in my innocence.

We scraped the roads, but the township's board insisted that they be tarred. We had been assured that the two wells on the property would provide adequate water. Again the township's board rejected this, and insisted on water reticulation from Rand Water Board – a costly affair. Finally the Electricity Supply Commission (ESCOM) charged us a large sum to install poles to run a current to our property from their nearest point.

The attorney-general had registered the property as 'Tileba' (after his three children – Tilly, Leon and Barbara). Tileba turned out to be a nightmare, particularly as the property market was in the doldrums.

It was only years later that we sold our last stand. We recovered our capital with a small profit –it was hardly enough to pay for my aspirins over the years. My second property flop! I began to wonder whether I was just a stupid property entrepreneur, or whether I perhaps did not have the right birdie on my shoulder. No wonder they say, 'Cobbler stick to your last.' I was learning the hard way. But I was never really interested in shoes!

In 1943 I made another sortie into the business arena. An old school pal and golfing mate had an important job with Transvaal Cold Storage. He was an expert on milk. One day he moaned to me that a wonderful snip had come his way. His firm's most important client in the eastern suburbs of Pretoria, the Economic Dairy, was in the market for a song – the owner was set on retirement. Jooste Hamman said that if he could only lay his hands on £4,000 he could buy the Economic lock, stock and barrel, including the valuable property situated on the main road of Burnett Street in Hatfield. I could see that it was a good buy, and knew that with Jooste in charge it would do well.

I again enlisted the sympathy of William Macintosh. Canny Scot though he was, he still had his heart in the right place – he owed me, as I had procured for him his directorship of the Provincial Building Society. He underwrote a bank overdraft of £4,000 for me.

I registered Economic Dairies (Pty) Ltd, gave Jooste 50% interest and bought the dairy. My 50% I shared with Brian, unbeknown to him aloft in the sky somewhere in North Africa.

Jooste Hamman immediately resigned from the Transvaal Cold Storage, and within months had Economic running smoothly and profitably. By the time that Brian returned to be demobbed, Jooste had already opened a branch dairy on the other side of the railway line in Arcadia. As far as I was concerned, this was more like it – no more aspirins and surely no more property development schemes for me – leave that to the agrarians! 'It was a far, far better thing I did than I had ever done.'

Before that fateful VE Day in Europe, I had my last experience outside the scope of accounting and auditing.

Soon Brian would be back in his old harness, Gibson and Rorke would throw off its wartime shackles, sport would again return to its organised formation and life once more would be happy, fruitful and rewarding. The trees in my Arcadia house were in full bloom, and everything in my garden was lovely. Little did I suspect!

The start of the war had so disorientated the organisation of sport, of rugby, cricket and hockey, that our small gang of reluctant key men agreed to take up golf. Clubs we bought, coaching lessons we took, and Murray Farm Golf Course we joined. Every Sunday became crammed with thirty-six holes, our bevy of beauties eagerly gazing at us from the cool of the pool, patiently awaiting our nineteenth hole, refreshment and evening dinner. This weekly ritual remained unchanged from year to year. The young girls' rapture when one fine day I introduced champagne at sundown was a joy to behold. The habit became ingrained, and to suit our pockets we devised a crafty deception. We would ourselves fetch the bubbly from the bar. On the tray we dispensed cheap tots of Witzenberg wine (2s 3d a bottle), and topped up each glass with lemonade and ice. A delicious home-brewed champagne, happily sipped in gratitude by our unsuspecting and adoring companions. And cheap!

Gradually, week after week, I felt my bond with Brian and Jooste becoming less firm. And then, as had been the wont throughout my life, there came another bombshell!

By some strange quirk of circumstance, I myself was at the time involved in a contretemps with my old pal and partner. Brian had returned to civilian life unused to the daily slog which is the lot of every practising accountant.

The exigencies of the war had turned me into a veritable

workaholic. Brian on the other hand had become accustomed to leisurely days between flights spent in comfort in military canteens – convivial glass and cigarette in hand. But life had now to change back to normal. Brian could not adapt. For six whole months I earnestly tried to coax him back into the office instead of spending hours drinking coffee at Turkstras. I am normally a patient man. But enough was enough! The work at the office was mounting up daily, and Brian's contribution was negligible. My ultimatum to Brian was adapt or go! We dissolved the partnership, and back I went to revive W B Rorke and Company. We agreed to split the clients and the partnership assets fifty-fifty. The tricky part was the half-shares in the Economic Dairy and Pretoria Enterprises, which I had bestowed upon Brian during the war.

These interests had to be divided equally. I ceded my Dairy share to Brian, while I retained his shares in Pretoria Enterprises. The Dairy was worth a hundredfold more than the Valhalla property. I suffered gigantic loss; for many years thereafter, the Dairy went from strength to strength. Its eventual sale provided its shareholders with sizeable pensions. 'Blow, blow, the winter wind' once again.

Before the war Brian, Jooste and myself, together with many others, had all been ex-scholars of Pretoria Boys High School. All our sport was conducted under the umbrella of PBHS Old Boys' Club. With the finish of the war the club agreed that a home had to be found for a new clubhouse.

Brian and I went on the committee that eventually purchased, at bargain price, ground in Lynnwood from Frank Struben and built the present club at Queen's Crescent.

I no longer played golf or hockey. I concentrated on tennis, and joined Pretoria Country Club. I served on the tennis committee and later became tennis captain. I also served on the general committee as chairman of finance. I rose to be chairman of the Country Club for three years. There was however a silver lining. Had I not broken with Brian I would perforce have had to include him in my flotation of Trek Airways.

The consequent watering down of my interests would have cost me far more than the loss which I sustained by the sacrifice of shares in the Economic Dairy. The race was not always to the swift!

In final reflection I realise that even though my darling wife had succeeded in upsetting many relationships with my old school friends on account of her rather volatile nature, without her I might never have ventured into flying. After all, it was her magnetism that in the first instance attracted Rodney Rooken-Smith and Sydney Excel to meet and to give birth to the hazardous child that we called Trek Airways.

At long last the war years had dragged on to their interminable end! Civilisation had stood still, but survived to see a brave new world arise, in which it became possible for enthusiastic men of vision to contemplate such a bold step as giving birth to Trek. And that was how I became involved in Trek Airways.

Obituary:
Friederich von Mellenthin,
Rommel's Chief of Intelligence

Written by Janice Farquharson[2]

Friederich Wilhelm von Mellenthin, the German officer best known for his association with Field Marshal Erwin Rommel in World War Two has died, aged 92, in Johannesburg. Although regarded as the 'Desert Fox's' chief of intelligence, von Mellenthin's career had far wider implications. He saw service on virtually all fronts, from the invasion of Poland and the conquest of France in 1940, to the Balkan campaign.

In June 1941 von Mellenthin joined Rommel's staff in the Western Desert, being invalided home in September 1942. From November 1942 to September 1944 he fought on the Russian front, before being recalled for the final encounters in the West with the Allies.

Von Mellenthin was born in Breslau, Silesia, on 30 August 1904. His mother was a direct descendant of Prince August of Prussia, a nephew of Frederick the Great. Paul Henning von Mellenthin, young Friederich's father, was killed in action on the Western front in 1918.

Von Mellenthin's mother brought up her three sons alone, a feat he later acknowledged, calling her 'my guiding star in peace and war'.

In 1924 von Mellenthin enlisted in the 7th Cavalry Regiment at the time when the provisions of the Versailles Treaty severely limited the strength of the German army. As only 4,000 officers' posts were available, promotion was slow, but von Mellenthin was ordered to report to the War Academy in Berlin for training in

---

[2] Reprinted with kind permission

1935. He displayed considerable powers of organisation and was responsible for ceremonial parades honouring visiting dignitaries, including Mussolini.

In March 1936 he had his hands full preparing a gigantic military parade to mark Hitler's 50th birthday.

However, he later wrote: 'I longed to get away from this sort of life. I was tired of running a military circus, and wanted to return to the troops.'

His wish was granted when he was posted to Panzer Regiment 5 in 1939. On 1 September of that year Germany invaded Poland.

Von Mellenthin ended the war as a prisoner of the Americans, spending two and a half years in captivity.

In the last weeks of the war he, like so many German soldiers, was tormented with anxiety as 'we all realised the horrible dangers facing our families in the East'.

He eventually learned that his family had escaped the 'Soviet hordes; luckier than many they saved nothing but their lives and a bundle of clothes they carried on their backs'.

His first wife, Ingeborg von Auloch, whom he married in 1932, had a grandfather, Malcomess, who had emigrated to South Africa. Thanks to these connections (and an inheritance from the grandfather), the family was able to immigrate to this country in 1954.

Here he joined Trek Airways as a shareholder and sales director. He was a man of managerial ability, and in 1961 Lufthansa appointed him director for Africa.

In 1955 he published *Panzer Battles 1939–1945: A Study in the Use of Armour in the Second World War*, a work of lasting value and interest, not only to military enthusiasts.

In it he expressed his admiration for Rommel. 'He was in my opinion the ideal commander for desert warfare by going himself to the danger spot, and he had an uncanny facility for appearing at the right place at the right time, he was able to adapt himself to new situations. What I admired most were his courage and resourcefulness and his invincible determination under the most adverse circumstances.'

Von Mellenthin was with Rommel at the capture of Tobruk, that defeat with such bitter memories for South Africans: 'The white flag was hoisted over General Klopper's Headquarters, and 33,000 prisoners fell into our hands at a single stroke. In spite of demolition, numerous dumps of food, petrol, clothing and ammunition were found intact, and many guns, vehicles and tanks swelled the booty of the Panzerarmee,' he wrote.

According to his family, von Mellenthin was deeply affected by – and, indeed, felt partial responsibility for – the division of Germany into East and West.

Von Mellenthin is survived by his second wife, Sybille, seven children, 19 grandchildren and nine great-grandchildren.

A Tribute to William Buckland Rorke (Paddy)

William Buckland was born 22 February 1915 in Witbank, a coal-mining small town fifty miles east of Pretoria. At the time of his birth his Uncle Jim said, 'I was expecting a girl. I don't what you are going to call him, but to me he will always be Paddy, "Paddy the next best thing"' – and Paddy he was then and for ever more. No one ever dared to call him William.

In 1925, at the age of ten, he started his secondary schooling at the Pretoria Boys High. Paddy matriculated at the age of fourteen. He then went to Rhodes University in Grahamstown to study for a B.Com degree, planning to become an accountant. But in 1931 Paddy was forced to return to Pretoria owing to the depression. Thus, at the beginning of 1932, he became articled with Price Waterhouse and Peat for six days a week. At the same time, he proceeded with his degree extramurally at the Pretoria University. In 1936, Paddy qualified as a chartered accountant with a B.Com degree, as well as being an associate of the Chartered Institute of Secretaries. In October 1987, he became an honorary life member in recognition for more than fifty years as a chartered secretary. He started work for Mr George Beckett at Beckett and Murray, a department store in Church Street, as an accountant. Shortly afterwards, he became an extramural lecturer at the Pretoria University and the Pretoria Technical College. In addition, he wrote a correspondence course for a private institution called the University Correspondence College.

In 1937, he started his own accountancy firm, W B Rorke & Company. This firm later became known as Gibson & Rorke in 1945, after he was joined by Brian Gibson, a school friend from Boys High, who had also qualified as an accountant. However, owing to the aftermath of the war, this was not a successful partnership and the partnership was dissolved. The firm then became Rorke & du Toit, finally reverting to W B Rorke & Co. He holds a record of being one of the oldest and longest practicing accountants in South Africa. He was still working up to the time of his death in July 2003.

In 1953, the concept of Trek Airways was born, and it became a household name for economy overseas travel. He was one of the founder directors, later becoming the company's chairman for twenty-five years. John Foggitt, founder of TFC Tours, used Trek/Luxavia for his famous TFC Tours all over the world. Paddy and Brian Gibson were instrumental in purchasing the ground in Queen's Crescent, Lynnwood for the PHSOB clubhouse and sports fields. He was chairman of finance for Pretoria Country Club Committee for many years. He was also chairman of the club for three years. Paddy was an all round sportsman – finally playing bowls at PHSOB. He was also an upstanding toastmaster for over twenty-five years. Paddy was one of the founder members for Toastmaster 2000, being the first club in Pretoria to admit ladies as toastmasters.

He is survived by his wife, Yvonne, and his daughter, Shane. His brother Bryan died in December 2004.

Requiem

The jetting crowds have all dispersed, the tumult and the shouting now died down. Whereas before no day seemed even long enough, today each day drags slowly to its dreary close – with memories of things that were, with thoughts of all things that are, and with dread of all things that still may lie ahead.

Now there is time for past reflections, for gratitude for things that were, and for regret of things that might have been.

One's thoughts go back to the road along which we at Trek all travelled – to those who pointed out the path, to those who had the wherewithal to start along the road, and to those whose energy, devotion and expertise brought us safely to the end of the journey.

Syd Excel was the man who alone showed us the way, and dragged us, though we were so hesitant, along with all his enthusiasm. How ironic was it then that just as we began to march ahead Syd himself should have been the first to leave the track, to disappear for ever from our ken. He was, indeed, a man to love, a man to hate, but still the pioneer of all our endeavour and of all our enterprise.

All hail to Sydney Excel!

Fanie Botha, as ever a man of fire and a bold adventurer, coerced us into action. He it was who led us forward with a spirit so indomitable as to brook no disillusion, to admit no sense of failing, with a drive that no one dared resist!

A supreme juggler of finance, with a silver tongue that could not but bend all others to his will. A man of stature! Albeit one whose feet in search of wealth and fame often turned to clay. In other circumstances, and with a more developed sense of honest purpose, he might well have carved for himself a niche amongst the men of fame in our South Africa.

Alas, poor Fanie, I knew him well!

Epilogue

It was to these two figures, each of a mould so different one from the other, that Trek remains indebted for the road – that long, long road that wound its way for more than a third of the twentieth century. To them we also owe the impetus to set our feet upon the path that led us eventually to our final destination.

How tragic then it was that both these characters should have stepped off the road within the first twelve months, and vanished completely – never to be heard of again! The road which they had so valiantly pointed out.

How fortunate that we who were left plodded on and on to reach our final goal. We were indeed throughout our progress urged on by the words that have so inspired many others over the years:

> Keep right on to the end of the road
> Keep right on to the end
> Tho' the way be long, let your heart be strong,
> Keep right on round the bend.
> Tho' you're tired and weary still journey on,
> Till you come to your happy abode,
> Where all the love you've been dreaming of
> Will be there at the end of the road.

We, who were left, arrived there. It was only after we had left, and gone to take our rest that those who followed strayed from the road, to end up in the desert from which no one can return!

Now have they all, all those who so faithfully followed along the road, gone to their last eternal flight with Father Time in the left-hand seat. 'To sleep, to sleep! Perchance to dream!'

Praestantia Prevalent – the new Republic of South Africa.

Printed in the United States
220340BV00001B/2/A